The Legend Behind Lenovo

The Chinese IT company that dares to succeed

Shan Feng & Janet Elfring

Asia 2000 Limited
Hong Kong

ISBN: 962-8783-31-9

Published by Asia 2000 Ltd
18th Floor, Hollywood Centre,
77-91 Queen's Road West, Hong Kong

http://www.asia2000.com.hk

Typeset in Goudy Old Style by Kashif Akhtar, Asia 2000 Ltd
Printed in Hong Kong by Yau Yee Printing & Binding Co.

First Printing 2004

Contents

Part 3 New Directions

Part 4 Passing the Torch

Part 5 Visions of the Future

Preface

I joined Legend* right after I graduated from university and had worked with the company for over a decade. Over the past 10 years, I have witnessed the drastic changes of the Chinese economy brought about by the open door policies adopted by the Chinese government. I have also experienced first hand, the founding, development and growth to full-fledge a commercial organization that now stands as one of the most outstanding companies in China, one that has ridden the immense tide of transformation within the country to reach global recognition and success. I am blessed with many touching moments and they are what urged me to share Legend's legendary story with others.

There is, however, another important reason for writing this book. Following China's accession to the World Trade Organization (W.T.O.), an increasing number of foreign companies have shown strong interest in understanding China's business environment; more and more research are being conducted with successful Chinese businesses as case studies. Yet, despite enquiries and search for information by international specialists, scholars, businessmen and investors, not a single publication on Legend's history and

---

* The company formally changed its name from "Legend Group Limited" to "Lenovo Group Limited" in April 2004. Since this book concerns itself with the group's history prior to the change of name, "Legend" shall live a little longer on these pages, giving way to "Lenovo" only in the final two chapters.

development has been compiled for non-Chinese readers. To remedy this situation is also another factor that inspired this undertaking.

Writing this book was not an easy task. First of all, China's market economy has come into existence for only slightly more than 20 years. There is little published research on Chinese enterprises and on the development of Chinese companies written from the Western point of view. The general lack of transparency that afflicts Chinese businesses and the language barrier as well did not help the understanding of Chinese enterprises by the Western world. Through my dealings with overseas companies in the past, I have discovered and am intrigued by the fact that they did not merely have problem understanding Chinese companies themselves, but also in understanding the history, culture and environment within which they exist. And it was the clear conveyance of business operations in such context that posed the greatest challenge to me as the writer, and at the same time, made me all the more convinced that the effort is worthwhile.

Through Danny Xiao, a friend who recently returned from the United States of America, I was introduced to Janet Elfring. In her thirty years of work in the United States, she spent six years as deputy press secretary for the governor of the State of Pennsylvania. With a bachelor's degree in Chinese history, she began teaching English in China in 1999. Janet has a lifelong interest in China and together we started on this book. For the past year, we have worked closely together. Because of our language and cultural differences, we have had many debates and sometimes argument, but we were able to ultimately reach mutual understanding and came to find our collaboration stimulating and creative. Together we did interviews, and discussed and wrote the stories.

We completed this book, but we know we could not have done it just on our own. We thank Legend's management and staff for their invaluable help and support throughout the entire process that has made it all possible. Special acknowledgments also go to Michael Morrow and Todd Crowell of our publisher Asia 2000, for their tireless efforts in providing us with valuable advice and comments on both the content and editorial style of the book.

This book would not have been written and published without the inspirations and invaluable reference provided by the many people we have talked with. We owe them and also the many other publications, including but not limited to, all Hong Kong and international newspapers and magazines, as well as academic case studies which have covered and written about Legend, the deepest respect and appreciation.

To cover 20 years of Legend's history in a short book meant that we had to condense a great deal of information. What have therefore been included in the book are key events and major milestones in Legend's development. We hope that by reading this book, you will be able to understand how a Chinese enterprise has grown, changed its value system and came to be hailed as a modern miracle by seizing the opportunities that have arisen as China transforms from a planned economy into a market economy.

Our work is now finished. We regret, however, that we are not able to include all the stories we gathered and people we talked to in the book. Still, we hope readers will find the contents of *The Legend Behind Lenovo* sufficiently rich, comprehensive and unique for contributing to international understanding of not only Legend/ Lenovo itself but also Chinese companies at large. If those goals are realized, this book will have served its purpose.

Shan Feng
Beijing, China

Lenovo at a Glance

Established: 1984

Headquarters: Beijing, the People's Republic of China (PRC)

Chairman: Liu Chuanzhi

President and Chief Executive Officer: Yang Yuanqing

Turnover: HK$23,176 million/US$2,971 million (FY2003/04)

Profit attributable to shareholders: HK$1,053 million/US$135 million (FY2003/04)

Business: Manufacture and sale of personal computers (including desktop computers and notebook computers), mobile handsets, servers and peripherals, etc.

Manufacturing bases: Beijing, Huiyang (Guangdong Province) and Shanghai, the PRC

Company website: www.lenovo.com

Major Milestones

1984

- The New Technology Developer Inc. (predecessor of Legend Group) was founded under the auspices of the Chinese Academy of Sciences.

1987

- Successfully rolled out the Legend Chinese-character card.

1988

- Legend's Chinese-character card received the highest National Science-Technology Progress Award.
- Legend Hong Kong was established as a distributor of major international branded computer products and peripherals (included those from IBM, AST and HP) in China.

1989

- Legend Hong Kong began to design and manufacture motherboards, and provide systems integration products and services for large corporate and government clients in the People's Republic of China (PRC).

1990

- Legend began to design, manufacture and distribute its own

Legend brand computers.

1992

- Legend pioneered the home PC concept in China. Legend 1+1 home PCs entered the Chinese marketplace.

1993

- Legend invested in Huiyang, Guangdong Province of China and built the Legend Science and Technology Park as the Group's manufacturing base.

1994

- Legend Hong Kong was listed on The Hong Kong Stock Exchange.
- Legend started to establish distribution networks and retail shops.

1995

- Introduced the first Legend-brand server.
- Young computer users in China rated Legend as their favorite national PC brand.
- Legend garnered 2nd place in the Top 100 Electronic Enterprises of China for the year.

1996

- Launched first own-brand notebook computer in China.
- Legend computers became the market-share leader in China for the first time.

1997

- Legend signed an Intellectual Property agreement with Microsoft,

the most valuable deal ever made in China at the time.
- Legend merged its businesses in HK and the PRC.

1999
- Legend became the top PC vendor in the Asia-Pacific region.
- Received the highest ranking in the Top 100 Electronic Enterprises of China.
- Launched first generation Internet PC, "Conet" with its "one-touch-to-the-net" feature.
- Joined forces with Microsoft to promote the Venus Project and develop the Internet market in China.

2000
- Legend was included as one of the constituent stocks of the Hang Seng Index and the London Hang Seng Reference Index.
- Legend ranked as one of the world's top 10 PC vendors.
- *BusinessWeek* ranked Legend 8th on its list of global Top 100 IT companies.
- Legend was named "The Best Managed Company in the PRC" by various investor relations magazines.

2001
- Yang Yuanqing was appointed President and CEO of Legend.
- Secretary-General Jiang Zemin and Vice Premier Li Lanqing visited Legend.
- Spin-off of Digital China from Legend and its successful listing on The Hong Kong Stock Exchange.
- Joint venture with America Online, Inc. (AOL) to develop consumer interactive service business in China.

2002

- Legend launched its first technological Innovation Convention, "Legend World 2002" during which the Group introduced its visionary "Collaborating Applications" concept for the future of technology development and applications.
- The joint venture with Xoceco was announced, marking Legend's formal entry into the mobile handset business.
- Invested in Han to jointly develop the IT management consultancy business in China.

2003

- Secretary-General Hu Jintao visited Legend.
- The birth of the new logo **lenovo联想**.
- Launched the most scalable technology roadshow, the "Lenovo Tech Show" in major cities in China to promote the concept of Collaborating Applications.
- The new manufacturing base in Shanghai commenced operations.
- Legend, together with Intel, announced the establishment of the Intel-Lenovo Technology Advancement Center in Beijing.
- Successfully rolled out new supercomputer "Deepcomp 6800" which ranked 14th among the world's top 500 supercomputers.

2004

- Became the first Chinese enterprise to join the Olympic Partner Programme of the International Olympic Committee.
- Formally changed the English company name from "Legend Group Limited" to "Lenovo Group Limited".

Part 1

The Birth of Legend

01. Stirrings

Anyone who visited China in 1984 would have detected the transformation that had come over the vast country. The political slogans and huge portraits of Mao Zedong and Karl Marx that once dominated the cityscape had been replaced by primitive billboard advertisements touting consumer products, some of them from the West. Free markets had sprung up in major cities, stocked with quantities of walnuts, celery, pumpkins, fresh fruits of all kinds, including staples such as chicken and pork. On the streets, you could see people beginning to wear clothes with bright colors and pastels, replacing drab grays, blues and blacks. In the major cities the few hotels that existed were full with foreign businessmen in pursuit of joint ventures with Chinese businesses.

More than five years had passed since the Chinese Communist Party, under the leadership of paramount leader Deng Xiaoping, had put the country on a new course, usually described as one of economic reform and opening up to the outside world. Change had proceeded in fits and starts; two steps forward and one step back. Powerful elements in the Party still opposed changes that put "cash in command", but by 1984 the results were becoming obvious and the course was firmly set. In the countryside, Deng had dismantled the agricultural communes set up by Chairman Mao. After meeting a government quota for food staples, farmers were free to grow whatever crops they wished on their own plots – the reason more produce was showing up in the market.

This book is about the birth and growth of the Legend Group, China's largest information technology enterprise, which has its origins in this same period. ("Legend" is a rough English rendering of "Lian Xiang", the name by which the group is known in Chinese. For future development reasons, the group's management has formally changed the company's English name from "Legend Group Limited" to "Lenovo Group Limited" in April 2004. Since this book concerns itself with the group's history prior to the change of name, "Legend" shall live a little longer on these pages, giving way to "Lenovo" only in the final chapters.) Beginning in 1979, Deng introduced a two-part industrial shape-up that was the most dramatic reorganization of Chinese industry since the founding of the People's Republic of China (PRC) in 1949. The first aspect of this strategic shift concerned the allocation of capital and other scarce resources; funds and focus would shift from heavy industry to neglected sectors of the economy such as energy, transportation and, most importantly, to consumer goods. Since the 1950s, China had concentrated on developing fundamental industries, focusing on such sectors as iron and steel, heavy machinery, aviation and armaments.

The second aspect of this shift concerned decision-making. In the past, everything had relied on planning and control that flowed from Beijing. Borrowing flexible market-oriented ideas from Eastern European countries that were still nominally socialist, factory managers would now be given the freedom to reinvest their profits as they saw fit rather than automatically turning them over to the appropriate ministry. Under the new "responsibility" system, the Chinese government would still own the company – thus maintaining the socialist ideal of state ownership of the means of production – but factory managers would be free to draw up their own production plans, market their products to whomever they could, set their own prices and adjust wages of their employees.

These reforms were meant to apply throughout the whole economy. A few companies, Legend pre-eminent among them, evolved into something entirely new: "state-owned, privately-run" companies where state overseer virtually disappeared. Even today, although it is run as if it were a capitalist enterprise, Legend's major shareholder is 65% owned by the state.

To understand the contemporary phenomenon, it is important to understand the watershed past. For Chinese scientists and engineers, the Deng reforms were like a second Liberation. The previous two decades had not been kind to scientists unless they were directly involved with the military or with one of Chairman Mao's pet projects. Intellectuals had been labeled as the "stinking ninth category"; they had suffered greatly during the Cultural Revolution (1967-1976), when many had been yanked out of their classrooms or laboratories and sent to the countryside to perform manual labor. Attitudes changed after Deng returned to power. At the National Science Conference in the spring of 1978, he proposed that the "intelligentsia" be deemed part of the "working class". That was an important statement since, under Marxist theory, the Communist Party represents the working class. It was a sign that the Party recognized and exalted the political status of scientists.

Scientists were now held in high esteem, and many were happy to ivory towers, producing research papers that were filed away and forgotten. On the other hand, mere businessmen, those who made their living through buying and selling, were still lowly by comparison. Technology had become one of Deng's four modernization programs, yet there was still no political or business culture to support scientist-entrepreneurs, not even the idea of entrepreneurship.

These changes were also being felt in the Zhongguancun area of Beijing's Haidian District, now known as "China's Silicon Valley". This once sleepy suburban village in the northwestern section of the city was home to many of China's most important research institutes and universities, including Peking University, Tsinghua University and several others, as well as several government research institutes. Among the institutions engaged in government-funded science and technology development, was the Chinese Academy of Sciences (CAS). At the time, it managed the work of 120 or so research institutes. CAS had contributed to the development of the national economy during the People's Republic of China's formative years, but because of its prolonged focus on academic and theoretical research, it had become divorced from the national economy.

A pioneer in turning CAS in a new direction was a researcher named Chen Chunxian. He had visited the United States three times, paying special attention to a strip of high technology start-ups along Route 108 near Boston. Inspired, he decided to set up a privately run "new technology department" along Zhongguancun Road. It was the first of many. One of the most important departments of CAS to get involved in such entrepreneurship was the Institute of Computing Technology (ICT). Founded in 1956, the Institute had played a key role in developing more than twenty mainframe computers, despite embargoes and other difficulties that prevented it from obtaining technology from abroad.

In 1982 the central government affirmed the critical role of science and technology in the development of the country. But at the same time it began to severely cut back on government funding. That year Zeng Maochao, one of the Institute's premier scientists, was appointed chief. Zeng had to find ways to raise the money needed to support the more than 1,500 people working at the Institute. At first he tried to commercialize research that might apply directly to some of China's heavy industries, and he got a few orders from the oil exploration industry. At the same time he encouraged some of the experienced researchers to start their own businesses. One of them was a 40-year-old talented researcher and administrator named Liu Chuanzhi, and it is here that the story of Legend really begins.

In 1984, Liu was also feeling the changes that were sweeping the country. Already approaching middle age, he had experienced many of the trials of his generation. He had been born in Shanghai in 1944 to a family with a long tradition in banking. His grandfather had been a banker, and his father, Liu Gushu had worked at the Bank of China, a "patriotic capitalist" working secretly for the Communist Party before Chairman Mao drove the Kuomintang out of China in 1949. After Liberation, the elder Liu helped re-establish the new Bank of China. He later became a lawyer and moved to Hong Kong to become a specialist in intellectual property law. As a young man, Liu Chuanzhi dreamed of becoming a fighter pilot. He passed the first round of selection and qualified for pilot training. But joining the Chinese Air Force in those days required political reliability as well as aeronautical skills. Despite his father's revolutionary credentials, Liu was disqualified from pilot training because his uncle was considered a "rightist". He enrolled in the Xian Military Communications Engineering College to study radar communications. After he graduated in 1967 he was caught up in the Cultural Revolution, the great convulsion that sent him, like many other college graduates, to the countryside to become a farm laborer.

In 1984, Liu had long returned from the rice paddies, but he was still a frustrated man. He was stuck as a computer scientist, earning only about RMB100 a month, and he had a growing family to support. More than that, he felt professionally stymied. He was doing important work on magnetic storage, but most of it was theoretical. "We were the top computer technology research organization in

China. We developed the first electron-tube computer and the first transistor computer. But we only produced one of each. Then we just went on to develop something else. The work was just filed away," he later recalled.

Meanwhile, Liu's superiors at CAS were feeling the impact of the new economic currents let loose by the reform. If the academy was to carry on its mission and bring science and technology into the national economy and maintain employment for scientists, it was going to have to turn its research into something practical. So the senior administrators approached Liu with an offer that would not only change his life but also ultimately have significant impact on China's corporate culture and business history. With some seed money from CAS, he and ten of his colleagues were asked to set up a separate business unit. His mission was as vague as the investment was small: to turn the institute's research into marketable products. The initial capitalization was RMB200,000 or about US$25,000. The company had an ambitious name: New Technology Developer Inc. It would be known as NTD for the next five years.

02. Early Days

On the corner of South Zhongguancun Street stands an undistinguished, one-story concrete bungalow. Today it is used mainly as a guardhouse. Occasionally visitors are taken to look at it, since it has taken on mythical proportions, the Chinese equivalent of the Silicon Valley garages that spawned the American computer industry. There was nothing mythic about the place back in 1984. "It was cold and unfinished," recalled Zhou Xiaolan, one of the original eleven founders of Legend. "We had to put our feet on the heaters to keep warm. We bought and repaired used furniture and moved it in ourselves. We painted the walls. We had only one telephone, and that one had to go through an operator. While that one phone was in use, nobody else could reach us. Another phone would cost two-months' wages to install, and we couldn't afford it." At least the rent was right. The institute let them use it for free.

It was in November 1984 when Liu and ten colleagues from the institute set about transforming their vague mission to commercialize its research into reality. There were no blueprints, no rules, and no guidelines. The government had enunciated a general policy of liberalization and reform but it was up to Liu and his colleagues to put it into practice. The legal structures and institutions that businessmen in the West took for granted hardly existed in China at the time. They would take years to develop – indeed, they are still evolving. Everyone was in the dark, from government officials at all levels, to the managers of state-owned enterprises, to would-be entrepreneurs. To paraphrase Deng Xiaoping, Liu and company had to grope their way forward; it was like crossing a river, one rock at a time.

The original founders, all scientists and technicians, knew nothing about markets. It wasn't simply ignorance of business fundamentals – Liu understood that he had to overcome a tradition, one that predated the founding of the Chinese Communist state even, that it was somehow wrong for members of the intelligentsia to sully themselves by making money. Indeed, many of the "businessmen" who answered to Deng Xiaoping's original call "to get rich" were a fairly disreputable lot. In the early 1980s entrepreneurs were mainly people who did not fit into the state-owned economic system. Most non-state commerce was small scale, dealing with basic commodities. Private businessmen tended to be unreliable giving the private sector itself a bad reputation. Liu Chuanzhi and his colleagues could see this on their own street. In the mid 1980s, Zhongguancun Street was known as "Electric Street"; its sidewalks had a kind of Wild West quality, a tone set by thousands of fly-by-night dealers who flocked to the area to cash in on China's interest in electronic technology, an interest that mirrored the craze for personal computers and other digital devices that was becoming a worldwide phenomenon. Most Zhongguancun businessmen had a hit-or-miss style, which soon gave the street its other nickname: "Swindlers Alley".

When Liu and his colleagues decided to market their Chinese-character insertion card at a computer exhibition in 1985, none of them wanted to sell it. "I'm an engineer, not a salesperson," was a frequently heard comment. Finally one woman volunteered. She was Hu Xilan, wife of Zeng Maochao, the chief of the Institute of Computing Technology (ICT). She was a professor as well as the director of a large-scale computer research team. At the exhibition, the visitors and customers saw an arresting sight. Among the young models and other pretty girls stood one short, middle-aged woman with gray hair who it soon turned out had a knack for selling. Customers responded to her knowledge and to her advice, which was sincere and in the customer's best interest. Even though Hu was a professor and wife of the chief, she set a fine example, and soon other scientists were willing to join the sales team.

Liu understood from the start that there was also more to their survival than learning how to "walk the talk" of Zhongguancun. It was essential that from the start they establish a proper working relationship with their superiors. Despite the rhetoric of reform, there remained the distinct possibility that the Institute would try to micro-manage his new company. After all, that was how things had been done in China since the Liberation. In addition, Liu would have to deal with local governments run by Communist Party cadres, especially the municipal administration of Beijing's Haidian District. "We were totally immersed in the environment of a planned economy," he said. "I didn't care that the investment was small, but I knew I must have control over finances, human resources and decision-making." Fortunately, both of Liu's immediate superiors at the time, Zeng Maochao, chief of ICT, and his boss, Zhou Guangzhao, the leader of CAS, were enlightened people. They readily granted Liu his request for independence.

These were the first in a number of decisions that would eventually make Legend the largest IT enterprise in China. Liu now likes to think collectively of those who gave him control over the company at that critical moment, including the Haidian authorities who also cooperated in legitimizing the company's independence, as an "enlightened mother-in-law". In old China every newly married woman had to submit totally to the control of her mother-in-law. Every bride hoped to have an "enlightened" mother-in-law, one who would allow her to run her own household. They were on their own.

The most advanced consumer products that the average Chinese consumer could hope to acquire then were a colored television set, a digital watch or maybe a washing machine. So for the first two years of its existence, Legend, still known as NTD, scrounged what business it could find wherever it could find it. It bought products from large state-owned importing companies and sold them to government agencies and other large state enterprises. It bought and sold whatever could be sold: digital watches, color televisions, skating shoes, pocket calculators, anything it could trade profitably. Liu opened a trading office in Beijing to sell American computers from IBM and the AST Corporation, printers from Hewlett-Packard and modems from Hayes. But it was difficult to compete legitimately with the many small distributors of smuggled products.

It was also difficult to recruit new people to join their little band. The planned economy was still very much in operation. The mentality that scientists should stay in the laboratory and do research remained strong. It took a leap of faith to give up cradle-to-grave state care, what the Chinese call the "iron rice bowl". And there were still considerable political risks in joining the new Legend-to-be. Who could say with confidence that China might not take another lurch to the extreme left? They might all be branded "rightists" and sent to re-education camps. Memories of the Cultural Revolution were still fresh. Liu wasn't the only one of Legend's founders who had been "sent down". And not being within the planned economy, they did not have a right to resources totally controlled by the government. If they wanted to make things, Legend's founders had to obtain a manufacturing license. It would take Legend eight years to get the coveted license to manufacture personal computers. Even though they wanted to import goods, they had no import quotas. It was difficult to get loans because state banks did not grant them to private enterprises. On the other hand, state-enterprises, which could manufacture things, could not freely engage in normal commercial activities. A state enterprise could, for example, apply for an import license and quota to buy foreign computers for their own use but not for resale. Thus they tended to re-sell their quotas and licenses at higher prices to companies like Legend, which could sell the computers. It was a cumbersome process. The main advantage that Legend enjoyed as a "privately-run" company was autonomy from government interference and independence in making decisions. That of course included the freedom to make mistakes.

Just one month after Legend was founded, the company learned there was a way to get import quotas for color televisions sets, which were then in short supply and thus commanding a high price. The Women's Union Commission, a shady outfit in Jiangxi Province claimed to have the necessary licenses. The newly minted entrepreneurs agreed to hand over RMB140,000 – nearly the entire initial investment in NTD. Liu recalled that when he returned from a business trip, it was too late to stop the deal. The middlemen disappeared with nearly all of Legend's money. Lack of cash would hurt Legend for several years. When Liu and his colleagues first ventured into Hong Kong, they went to an important meeting at a luxury hotel by public bus. After the meeting, they were escorted to the front door. To keep up appearances, Liu grandly called for a taxi, but having no money to pay for it, he and his colleagues promptly got out around the corner and took a bus. Still, even in its first year, Legend managed to turn a profit of RMB900,000 (about US$108,000).

All regulations then in existence were designed to support the planned economy, not private enterprise. Many things Legend did could be interpreted as "deviations". Beijing's Haidian District, from where the company did business, became a special enterprise zone in 1988. Technically, this meant that companies established there could sell their products free of price controls for three years. Nevertheless, one of the cadres in the municipal government thought Legend's prices were too high, and fined them RMB400,000. Many of the staff wanted to take the office to court, but Liu argued that they had to live in Haidian, and if they antagonized the municipal government by going to court, their local "mother-in-law" would cause them more difficulties in the future. Legend paid the penalty. The national policy of economic reform and an opening to the outside world was still fresh. The future offered ample opportunity for misunderstandings and every lesson of the past suggested a need to keep focused on the tasks ahead.

Of course, adversity also engendered a strong sense of dedication. The term constantly used by the founders to describe their motivation is "chuangye jingshen", or "pioneering spirit". By this they meant that they were willing to undertake any challenge. They were "pioneering spirits" at heart, and from the perspective of nearly two decades, they can now look back on the early days with nostalgia – and pride. They knew each other well, and they had been personally selected by Liu because he thought they had the drive and spirit needed to leave the security of ICT and take that leap into the unknown. They had all suffered in the ten years when the universities had been closed and many had been sent, like Liu, to the countryside to learn from peasants. When the Cultural Revolution ended, they all felt a tremendous pent-up energy as well as a genuine sense of patriotism to build a new China. Deng Xiaoping's call for reform inspired them and gave them an outlet to develop their country and advance themselves professionally.

At the beginning, there was no appreciation for the ways of business. So Liu began to make rules. For instance, if anyone was late for a meeting, he or she was made to stand silently in front of the group for however many minutes they were late. This was pretty severe in a country that values "face" as much as China does. Unexpectedly, one of the people who arrived late was Liu's former boss at ICT. Liu respected him and was a little unsure how to handle the situation. But in order to uphold the new rule, Liu said to him, "Please stand for a minute now. Then I'll go to your home and stand for a minute for you too."

The founders did not know then that their future depended on making computers. They only had a vague notion of transforming technology into products. In China there is a phrase, "xia hai", which means "jumping into the sea" literally leaving the state sector. They were stepping into the unknown. In the early 1980s, a market for computers hardly existed in China beyond the Zhongguancun-like street markets that had sprung up in a few Chinese cities. During the previous decades, China had been isolated from the outside world and closed to foreign imports. Other countries restricted exports to China, especially sensitive technologies such as computers, which had military applications. Indeed, most early computers had been developed for the military to use in helping design rockets and nuclear weapons. Most Chinese scientists and engineers labored in the dark, buying components where they could, designing their own machines. In 1973 the Ministry of Electronics Industries (MEI) had started to develop computers for civilian uses, but the numbers were very small. In the early 1980s, as China began to open to the outside world, MEI began importing some production lines. Still, computer technology did not figure strongly in the government's successive five-year plans during those years and state investment, at approximately RMB1.4 billion, was relatively small. China's computer industry had not achieved anywhere near the scale of manufacturing, marketing or service found in the West. The quality was poor, and quotas and high tariffs restricted imports.

This was the decade when computer technology came into its own in the West. The year Legend was founded, computer sales reached $46 billion – the computer giant IBM alone accounted for $23 billion. About the same time Microsoft went public with one of the largest initial public offerings in history. At the high end, third- was giving way to fourth- and even fourth to fifth-generation computers; meanwhile, all computers were getting smaller and operating systems were becoming standardized. As the decade progressed, the Chinese government began to put more emphasis on computers and related technologies. Preferential tax policies were adopted to steer more funds into research and development and manufacturing. The MEI approved some 161 new enterprises; Great Wall, then the largest domestic producer, obtained subsidy from MEZ. By 1991 the value of total production had risen to RMB6 billion (still only 0.3 percent of the worldwide output). Not being a part of the MEI family, Legend did not benefit directly from the government's preferential tax policies and direct subsidies. But the new emphasis on computers did lay the foundations for the Chinese computer industry and for a larger and more sophisticated domestic market within which a fledgling Legend could find its way.

A third to a half of all foreign computers imported into China were actually smuggled into the country at that time. Avoiding the tariff, they could be sold at much cheaper prices than legitimate brands. Many small distributors quickly sprang up along Electric Street to exploit the situation, muscling out of competition anyone who wanted to remain within the law. Former vice-president Li Qin, who was then responsible for marketing, remembers, "Compared with the other companies on Electric Street, Legend was clearly of a different character, with a high technology background and a trustworthy reputation. Our salesmen were not like the flashy-dressed young men working for other companies. We were scientists in our 40s, in simple clothing, and the customers could see our trustworthiness in our faces. This was a big factor in allowing us to get big orders from big customers, especially from government customers."

Legend's first tentative step in the direction of its future business came when it won a contract to test, install and maintain 500 IBM computers for the Chinese Academy of Sciences. The contract was worth RMB700,000 and was the first real money the company had a chance to earn. Liu and his colleagues quickly decided to plow it all back into the company. Liu had his sights to the south, toward Shenzhen, the Hong Kong border city that had recently been declared a Special Economic Zone (SEZ). Shenzhen had more liberal rules governing commerce and foreign trade. They would take advantage of these to import more foreign computers. But once again the importing agency took their money and ran. It took Liu and company three months to find the swindler and retrieve the money.

This contract would have far-reaching implications for Legend's future. Simply being a middleman was not the way. But what could they manufacture?

03. The First Success

In the 1980s, English was the dominant language of PC operating systems. Their alphanumeric keyboard and difficulty in transmitting Chinese characters onto the screen were major turn offs for users. The latter issue in particular perplexed the Chinese computer industry including the scientists at Legend. In 1986, to resolve the problem, the Chinese government launched the "Chinese Character Processing Project" and the Peking University High Technology Corporation, the predecessor of Peking Founder, which is now the second-largest PC maker in China, was set up specifically to take on the project. The market saw the first Chinese language publishing software in 1989. There were other companies including the American software giant Microsoft which were also laboring on appropriate software solutions.

Instead of software products, Legend decided to develop new hardware. Taking advantage of its close relationship with the Institute of Computing Technology (ICT), Legend borrowed a group of scientists who were researching a Chinese operating system under research director Ni Guangnan. The result was the Legend Chinese Insertion Card, to be inserted in computer motherboards. The insertion card used a pattern-recognition technology or "association" that enabled the user to input words and be prompted for characters or common phrases that were associated with that character. For example, one might enter the word "science" and receive prompts for "scientist" or "scientific", or even common phrases built on the word. The Chinese word for "association" is *lian xiang*, which also connotes "imagination". The device came to be known as the Chinese Association – or Lian Xiang – Card. Pronounced "li-en-siang", *lian xiang* is a rough homonym for "legend" in English. The Legend insertion card had several advantages over the immature Chinese software available at the time. It did not take up valuable hard disk space, and it could not be pirated. It was to be Legend's first big success. The next year the company received the National Science-Technology Progress Award, the nation's highest award for scientific progress. Such recognition allowed Legend to attract more talented engineers and scientists, who had earlier been reluctant to join a "privately-run" enterprise. And to capitalize on the continuing success of its profitable product, New Technology Developer Inc. changed its name to Legend in 1989.

The success of the Chinese insertion card also gave a boost to the distribution side of the company's business, since bundling the card with imported foreign computers made them more saleable in China. Legend's distribution business began in 1985 when it moved from providing post-sales services for IBM computer users to selling them their computers in the first place. Soon the company was selling IBM super personal computers with the Chinese card and providing service for its customers. But the distribution side of the business only began to make real headway in 1987 when the company signed agreements with the American computer-maker AST and with Hewlett-Packard. In particular, it started selling CAD (Computer Aided Design) systems for Hewlett-Packard a business that it was gradually able to expand into printers and other peripheral products.

Chen Xiaoming was only 25 when he took over the Hewlett-Packard (HP) operation. Just graduated from engineering school, he was working for a company called Shogu, one of the dozens of small companies that were springing up along Electric Street. In 1986, Shogu and 19 other firms merged with Legend. Chen remembers that he and the other scientists were not happy at all to join Legend, which then was much smaller than Stone or the other new technology firms popular at the time. They dragged their feet for several months until ICT finally forced the merger. Chen worked for about six months selling the insertion card and then was put in charge of distributing HP products in China. "At first the relationship was terrible," he recalls. "Communication was difficult, and there seemed to be no real common ground." The Legend people, being engineers predominantly, wanted to learn all they could from the American giant, and at first they were puzzled that HP's people had no desire at all to share such information. "We wanted to talk about technology; they wanted to talk about marketing. They were there purely to make money." He remembers how at one time a CAD player arrived broken from Spain. Legend's engineers wanted to repair it themselves but the Americans insisted that the machine be shipped back to Palo Alto. Thus, Legend comes to understand something of the concept of proprietary information.

There were plenty of other lessons to learn. The Chinese did not fully understand why the Americans concentrated exclusively on the bottom line. Of course, they knew vaguely that anyone in business had to make money. But making money was still something of an abstract notion for them. "The Westerners did not get so emotionally involved. They were not so concerned with face; business was business," recalled Chen. Legend didn't learn very much about technology from HP, but it learned something vastly more important for its future: modern business management techniques. From HP, Legend learned to be more sensitive to the market and to market trends, and it learned the value of working with established procedures. Because of its closer connections, Chen's nine-person department became much better organized than other segments of the growing company, using procedures that gradually permeated Legend's corporate culture as a whole. Other departments just talked among themselves. At his department, they wrote things down. "Of course, in my department it was easier to write things down because we had laser printers," Chen joked. In spite of the cultural differences, the relationship was successful from the start. By 1987 the company was already the leader among HP's five Asian agents outside of Japan.

It did not take a lot of market research to understand that the major buyers in China for imported computers and the other product lines they handled were the large state-owned enterprises (SOEs). In the 1980s there were scarcely any other kinds of customers. Legend was a state-owned company too, of course, but a different kind of SOE. Unlike the state-operated behemoths, Legend received no government subsidies. Even the initial grant of RMB200,000 was minimal compared with other government-aided start-ups. It had no special tax breaks or relief from the rather large import duties. If they wanted to import foreign products, Liu and his team had to obtain a license from one of the state import firms. Indeed, in those years the authorities usually ignored Legend. It wasn't until the early 1990s that the company finally gained the respect and attention of major ministries. But even before that, Legend was already poised to make another move.

04. The Move to Hong Kong

By the late 1980s, Legend had moved beyond its early teething problems, but it was still just one of hundreds of enterprises along Electric Street. It had not broken out of the pack. The engineers at Legend were eager to begin making their own computers, but they were stymied in their attempts to obtain a license to manufacture them. Other companies had better *guanxi* - connections. A direct offspring of the Ministry of Electronic Industries received one of the coveted licenses to manufacture and distribute its own branded computers in China while Legend did not. But in some ways the failure was a blessing, since, leaving aside some key parts. That company was required to buy most of its components in China and most of the local vendors were new and lacking in effective quality control. It could only sell to captive markets given to the Ministry.

Liu and his colleagues inevitably looked south, towards Hong Kong, then still a British colony. After all, many Chinese companies were beginning to migrate to this commercial outpost in search of markets and expertise that China could not yet provide, just as many foreign multinational corporations were settling in Hong Kong to try to penetrate the growing Chinese market. In 1988 Legend incorporated as Legend Hong Kong (effectively splitting the parent Legend Group Holdings into two branches: Legend Beijing and Legend Hong Kong). Zhang Zuxiang was placed in charge and would remain as head of the Hong Kong operations for eight years.

In Hong Kong, Legend quickly established joint ventures with Daw Computer Systems Limited, a Hong Kong trading company, and with China Technology Trade (H.K.) Limited and two other well-connected Chinese companies. Several young graduates of Great Britain's Imperial College of Science and Technology had founded Daw. They already had experience in international business and had, significantly, forged a relationship with AST. However, they lacked a strong technical base. Legend had a strong technical base but was a babe in the woods when it came to understanding overseas markets or international business rules. Looking back, Liu characterized the relationship as "the blind carrying the lame". As a young company then, Legend didn't know much about overseas markets and international business rules, which made it "blind". Daw lacked technology, manpower and production skills, so it was "lame". But Daw did have experience in international business and China Technology had money. Thus Legend's strong technology "legs", Daw's bright business "eyes" and China Technology's "purse" made for a powerful combination. Already, in 1989, Legend Hong Kong's first year in business, the Hong Kong operation had a HK$120 million turnover.

China Technology would soon separate from Legend Hong Kong, but the relationship with Daw would prove longer lasting and bring Legend into closer contact with AST. Legend became AST's exclusive agent in China. Before joining with Legend, AST had had to handle all of the cumbersome import procedures by itself, translating documents from Chinese into English and vice versa. Legend Hong Kong took over, handling the contract negotiations and the import and export routines while Legend Beijing handled distribution, sales and service on the mainland. Both sides benefited enormously. The partners increased sales and expanded the market, while Legend established and enlarged its distribution channels and increased its business. Before hooking up with Legend, AST had trailed both IBM and HP in the China market. With Legend's help, it vaulted into first place, for a while becoming the top PC vendor in China.

Even though its distribution business was growing rapidly, Legend still hankered to manufacture its own products. That, after all, was the main reason for moving to Hong Kong. The first step towards this goal occurred in late 1988 when it acquired a small motherboard manufacturing company called Quantum Design International (QDI) and began making motherboards for distribution overseas. At that time products from Taiwan dominated the market. QDI had only about 30 people most of whom were engaged in research. For the first three years the venture lost money, as Liu insisted on maintaining low prices as well as improving quality in order to gain recognition and eventually market share.

When the move to Hong Kong was decided in the mid-1980s, it was still difficult to make and sell products in China; in manufacturing its insertion card, for example, Legend often received poor quality components locally. The company leaders believed that in moving to Hong Kong, they would get better prices by doing business directly with suppliers, and that they would have better access to technical information. Component prices were always volatile, but at least by being in Hong Kong they could react quicker to changes in the market place. Still, at this stage Legend had little experience and no insulation from mistakes. Even in Hong Kong, it proved difficult to negotiate with overseas suppliers directly. As a small company, Legend could not get good prices even if it dealt with big vendors directly. In practice, Legend had to turn to smaller dealers. It paid US$160 per chip only to watch as the price plummeted to US$57. But at least Legend's leaders learned to know the market and not to hold a large inventory of parts.

This strategy eventually paid off. By 1995 Legend had established some thirty sales offices to market its motherboards and had become the fifth largest manufacturer in the world. When Legend's leaders look back on their early Hong Kong experience, it is not their distribution or manufacturing successes that they remember first. Being in Hong Kong was a major step towards Legend becoming a competitive business venture. "The mainland was so isolated then, that just going to Hong Kong was like opening a window to the world and letting the fresh air in," recalled Zhou Xiaolan, one of the original eleven, who later moved to Hong Kong as a manager. That does not mean that the move was easy. Just getting a visa to go abroad required lengthy checks by the security departments and the local foreign affairs branches. Even language presented a problem. "At first when we tried to buy supplies, we had to speak in Cantonese (the local dialect of Hong Kong and southern China). We had an assistant to interpret for us from Mandarin into Cantonese," recalls Zhou. "I even started trying to learn Cantonese in the evening. Later, we realized that they wanted our business, and it was up to them to learn Mandarin."

"Our clothes were from the mainland, and they were recognizably different from Hong Kong clothes," said Zhang. People immediately characterized them as "robes" from the mainland and made snide comments. Liu's father, who was then working in Hong Kong as an attorney, recommended that the Legend people simply buy clothes from local shops, but that was easier said than done considering the salaries they were making. Beijing still imposed limits on mainlanders' salaries. That meant a Chinese manager making a mere HK$1,000 a month even as his Hong Kong counterpart was taking home fifty times as much. Eventually the ceiling was lifted to HK$10,000 and a clothing allowance was added. Although the mainlanders still lagged far behind their counterparts for the most part, morale remained high. Says Zhang: "Personal development had to go hand-in-hand with the company's development. We were entrepreneurial spirits developing the country." Legend wasn't the only Chinese computer company to move to Hong Kong during those years, but it was one of a few to stay the course. Other Chinese companies could not shift out of their mainland mindset so failed to make the transition successfully. Legend alone was able to acquire and train good people and thus make the Hong Kong experience a crucial episode in the development of the company.

In eight years Legend had grown from its humble beginnings into a sizeable corporation. It had established profitable distribution businesses, invented the Legend Chinese Insertion Card and made its first serious foray into computer-related manufacture through its motherboard operation in Hong Kong. But it was not yet making computers.

In 1988, Liu and Ni Guangnan attended the world's largest computer exhibition, held annually in Las Vegas. There were still no Chinese products at the exhibition and Liu and company returned home, more determined than ever to make a successful Chinese PC. The model they chose was the 286PC, the standard second-generation Intel86-driven personal computer. First developed in 1982, the 286PC was still very much in demand even though faster, more powerful versions were already superseding it. They resolved to make the best quality machine possible using the latest technologies and strongest components. Their machine would be superior to the medium and low quality PCs then on the market in China yet sell for less than the imports. In Chinese terms, Liu would sell top vintage *Mao Tai* at ordinary *Er-guo-tou* prices. Legend's scientists worked feverishly in order to have a Legend machine available for display at West Germany's Hanover world's fair just three months hence. They hurried the first model to Beijing, only to have it held up by red tape at customs. It took a considerable amount of patriotic pleading to convince the custom officials to let the scientist with his sample enter the country on the eve of the Chinese New Year. By March 5, 1989, experts at Legend pronounced the machine ready in all respects and five days later the first mass-produced PC to be designed, manufactured by a Chinese company was introduced to the world in Hanover, Germany.

On the first day of the Hanover fair, about one thousand units were sold. Tens of thousands were sold over the next four days to customers from the United States and Europe. More significantly, the sales dissolved any objections that the Chinese government might have had about granting Legend the critical license it needed to manufacture computers in China. The Ministry of Electronic Industries and several others had sent a delegation to the fair and were impressed enough with what they saw to send another group to Hong Kong to examine Legend's manufacturing capabilities more closely. Satisfied, the ministry granted the coveted license in 1990.

An auspicious beginning, but Legend would face many hurdles before its managers could say they were really in the computer manufacturing business. And the first big challenge would come a lot sooner than they expected.

Part 2

The PC Wars 1992-1997

05. Foreign Competitions

Yang Yuanqing was only 25 with a newly minted master's degree in computer science from the University of Science and Technology of China when he joined Legend's research department in 1989. His earliest interests were literature and poetry, and he was still torn between business and teaching as a career. He had wanted to be a scholar, and his professor advised him to stay in academia, but he also felt that Legend would offer him more opportunities, especially a chance to study abroad. In comparison with many of the other young people then joining Legend, Yang stood out as being quiet but serious, a deep thinker, and he quickly caught the eye of Chairman Liu. Very soon Liu put him in charge of the Hewlett-Packard products distribution department, succeeding Chen Xiaoming.

Yang had planned to study abroad during the 1990 school year but Liu persuaded him to stay behind. Liu argued that he could learn more from the close association with the American company; he also promised that Yang could study abroad two years hence. Yang threw himself into the job but when the time came Liu could not live up to his promise. In the two years that had passed, Legend had again fallen on hard times, Liu had a much more important task for the serious young man.

In the 1980s, under the leadership of Deng Xiaoping, China had immersed itself in economic reform. Central to its opening to the outside world, Beijing had sought to be reinstated as a member of the General Agreement on Tariffs and Trade (GATT), which Chairman Mao Zedong had abrogated years before. In 1986, a panel began a serious review of the Chinese economic system focusing on whether China would stay a planned economy or continue to evolve in the direction of a market economy. During those years the average tariff on imports was more than 43 percent, the duty on electronic products even higher. It would take several more years, and much more negotiation, before China qualified to join GATT's successor, the World Trade Organization. But before that happened, Beijing and Washington in 1992 entered into a series of bilateral negotiations that would have enormous consequences for the development of a computer industry in China. The two countries concluded a Memorandum of Agreement reducing tariffs on hundreds of commodities. Beijing agreed to lower import duties on a broad range of products and Washington agreed to lift all of the trade sanctions against China imposed in 1989. The duty on imported personal computers fell from 50 percent to 20 percent, and other tariffs on software and electronic commodities were reduced accordingly. Along with reducing tariffs, many non-tariff barriers such as import quotas and license fees were eliminated.

The impact of these tariff reductions hit the heavily protected Chinese computer industry with the force of a typhoon. Suddenly big-branded American computers could compete on price with Chinese machines. These computers had considerably more computing power and the companies behind them more promotional experience, more after-sales service. Foreign-brand computer products entered the Chinese market one after another. Virtually overnight these products came to dominate the market. In 1992 some 70 percent of computer sales came from Chinese manufacturers. In the next year, 67 percent of total sales were from foreign companies. Electric Street felt like it was under siege. Too many Chinese companies had been coasting along in a protected market. Taking advantage of official policy to encourage local production, they were selling overpriced but underpowered machines to government offices and state-owned enterprises. Great Wall, despite its impeccable "connections", stopped producing its own brand of computer temporarily. Others did so too. By 1995 the strongest selling computer in China was the American-made Compaq. In retrospect, the invasion brought long-term benefit to the Chinese computer industry, but the adjustment was hard. "Before 1990, the market was small. Yearly turnover was about 100,000 units. The arrival of more foreign computers greatly expanded the market and helped us develop new applications. But in the meantime the national computer industry was almost destroyed," said Liu.

Like its compatriots, Legend was not ready for the onslaught and very nearly gave up the computer business. It had begun to sell its own computers after obtaining a manufacturing license in 1990. But after making a big splash at the 1989 Hannover World's Fair, progress had been slow. In the fateful year of 1993 Legend sold only about 20,000 computers, failing to meet its target by 30 percent. Despite a home court advantage, the company was not properly organized to compete with the big-time American brands. The company had long outgrown its two-room premises on Zhongguancun Street but was still a long way from being a mature competitor.

In the 1990s, more young people were brought into the company who did not share a common background with the original founders and did not fit easily into the corporate culture. The head of the Corporate Development Department, a very ambitious man, sought to build his own empire within Legend by extending control over various departments. Connected with organized crime, he also tried to control finances. Eventually he was sent to prison. Many of the older scientists still carried with them the engrained idea that science was more important and prestigious than commerce. They felt that technology should drive the company, especially investment in hardware, drawing on the success of the insertion card. Liu felt strongly that Legend was a business, and that profit should drive the company. Technology was only one part of the overall mix that went into producing that profit. The board of directors supported Liu's view. They firmly supported Liu's vision: trading, manufacturing and technology together were the proper strategy. Liu explained that as a developing company, Legend was simply not strong enough to compete directly with developed high-technology companies. It had to rely on fundamentals of marketing and manufacturing. Later it could develop proprietary technologies according to the market needs.

But if Legend could not compete on equal terms with the more developed companies, what should it do? The internal strife coupled with the drop in profits resulting from the intensive foreign competition put Liu in the hospital. From his sick bed, Liu did a considerable amount of soul-searching. One option of course was simply to stop making its own branded computer, leave the field to the foreigners while concentrating on the profitable distribution side. Liu knew that to cope effectively with the foreign onrush, his company needed more than just a "Made in China" label plastered on his machines. But if the Legend machines were not as sleek as the Western imports, they could at least be tailored to Chinese users and they could be made to fit the Chinese pocket book. "We spent a lot of time finding out whether a locally branded PC could have any advantage over foreign ones and what these strengths were. After a thorough study and exhaustive discussions we decided that a Legend brand could succeed." But first Liu needed to address Legend's internal problems. Others might tinker with the product; Liu decided he had to reengineer the company.

06. Re-Engineering

The first major decision Chairman Liu made was to put the 29-year-old Yang Yuanqing in charge of Legend's PC computer operations and give him a mandate to restructure the corporation. In the previous two years, Yang had benefited greatly from his close association with Hewlett-Packard. He had learned how to train people, how to distribute products, how to be an agent. From HP, he learned more about bundling computers with peripherals. He also studied HP's business model and management ideas in general. "I had been observing Yang for a long time before I appointed him to take over the PC business," recalled Liu. "He had clear goals, was broad-minded and straightforward. We trusted him." Liu was taking a risk to appoint someone so young to such a responsible position. Yang was less excited about the extraordinary promotion than one might think. He still harbored some disappointment over the lost opportunity to study in the U.S. Moreover, the power that Liu was planning to entrust to the younger man was unprecedented in Legend's history.

Yang's colleagues thought him both strict with others and immodest about himself. For sure, he was honest and straightforward to the point of being blunt. Sometimes people were afraid to enter into his office. Yang would eventually have to learn a more cooperative management style but for the moment there was no time. Before anything else, he would have to make some serious decisions. Yang's first major decision as general manager was to completely restructure Legend's computer business. When he took over, Legend's PC operations were organized along functional lines. Separate vice presidents were in charge of purchasing, manufacturing and marketing. Each area was evaluated by its ability to meet targets set in the annual planning process. This seems straightforward but it leads to problem, such as the failure to take full advantage of a fall in component prices. At the beginning of 1993, the purchasing department obtained components at five percent below budgeted prices. However, the information was not shared with the manufacturing and marketing teams but used by the department to hedge against failure to meet its own budget target. As a result, final products were sold at originally planned prices putting the company in a disadvantaged price position to its competitors'. Such behaviors were typical of state-enterprises then, and it harmed both the business and image of the company.

In his analysis, Liu had identified uncoordinated internal decision-making as one of the company's main weaknesses. With restructuring, all PC-related businesses were consolidated into a new "Personal Computer Business Unit" with Yang as general manager. Yang was given full command on the purchasing, manufacturing and marketing of all products and had final say on strategies in relation to new product launches, channel selection and pricing. Under the new regime, departmental managers would be evaluated not only on how their departments met departmental goals but how they contributed to the overall profitability of the business unit as a whole.

Yang also gradually introduced job descriptions that clearly defined each individual's responsibilities, and with them a system of performance evaluations on which each staff member's annual bonus would be determined. At that time, state enterprises distributed bonuses equally. There was also little sense of personal responsibility. Workers were traditionally passive, waiting for superiors to give them instructions. Yang thought differently, realizing that the overall performance of a company could be hindered by its weakest link. It was like a wooden pail. The shortest slat determined how much water the pail could hold. In order to enhance a company's overall performance, management had to identify and strengthen the weakest link; the shortest slat had to be replaced with a longer piece.

Next, Yang tackled distribution. Selling products throughout China is a very complicated process. The country is vast and fragmented, with economic conditions varying greatly from place to place. In many parts of the country in the early 1990s the infrastructure needed just to deliver computers to consumers hardly existed or was very primitive. Many of the local governments had their own policies and regulations. In order to do business, one had to deal with many different people, and different kinds of people, face-to-face. Customer relations was hugely important and organizing sales a continuous challenge.

Demand for Legend's Chinese Insertion Card had fallen off markedly after Microsoft introduced new software designed to use mainland China's simplified Chinese characters. This meant that Legend was depending more and more on personal computer sales to maintain profits. It also meant that other units besides the PC unit naturally wanted to sell computers too. These were creating internal friction and conflict.

At that time, Legend had already established a sizeable distribution network for distributing well-known and popular foreign-brand products. However, most of the distributor who were selling these foreign-brand products did not have much confidence in the new Legend products. Yang's solution to all of this was to establish a separate distribution and retail channel for its own computers.

Up until then, Legend had used both direct sales and a distribution network. Drawing on his experience in selling HP products, Yang decided to eliminate the company's direct sale of its personal computers entirely and to switch to independent distributors across the board. To sell directly necessarily involved a large, expensive sales team. It was very time-consuming to build and maintain such a countrywide network. In contrast, local distributors had their own relationships and had established their own local customer network, providing more convenient services.

Before1994, Legend's sales machine comprised more than 100 sales representatives and several hundred distributors. Yang shook it up and trimmed the sales force down to only 18 people, just adequate for managing a distribution network. Setting up an effective distribution network proved to be a tough task. Legend's brand was not then established, and its image could not compete with foreign brands in the marketplace. Legend took three major steps to gain the distributors' confidence. It promised to provide multiple products with the latest technology of the highest quality, a reasonable pricing system and a market supervising system. It promised to look out for distributor interests – in contrast with foreign vendors who tended to squeeze distributor's margins. And finally it promised to share Legend's success as well as the risks inherent in handling its products.

Wang Gang, one of the 18 sales executives, remembers a memorable trip to southwest China. "When Yang and I went to Chengdu, not one of the eleven companies there would become our distributor. Some of them even asked Yang whether he would let them distribute HP products, instead. We walked along almost every street in Chengdu and even learned to speak a little of the dialect. Finally we found one, the Guangling Company. It was very small, occupying a mere ten-meter office. But now it is our number one Chengdu distributor." In 1994, Legend sold 450 units in the city; a year later the number rose to 3,000.

In its distribution network, Legend evolved what it called the "Grand Legend" concept. This meant that independent distributors were considered as part of the Legend family. Legend shared information with them and rewarded their participation in its success. Distributors were trained to Legend's standards. When necessary, Legend brought in Microsoft, Intel or other foreign partners to assist in the training. In this way, distributors absorbed not only technological and product knowledge but also something of the company's management philosophy. Legend set up a system to evaluate not only distributors' sales performance but also their inventory, cash flow, service, compliance with pricing strategies, ability to gain customer feedback and other aspects of the business relationship. Many distributors grew up with Legend, some to become the largest computer distributors in their areas. As a group, they came to constitute a valuable source of customer information and one of the company's most valuable assets.

Today when analysts examine the sources of Legend's success, aside from the company's technology and its ability to design and tailor products for Chinese users, they cite its extensive distribution system, and the marketing and after-sales service that supports it. These enduring characteristics, which became the foundation of Legend's later success, can be traced back directly to Yang's reforms after the disastrous year of 1993.

Given China's political and economic environment at the time, building such an extensive, efficient and loyal distribution network can now be seen as one of the cornerstones of the company's success. But at the time other problems kept Yang from complacency. Yang turned his attention to controlling costs. Here the most important element was management of inventory and close control over accounts receivable. Once more something that might be considered second nature to mature corporations in capitalist countries had to be learned almost from scratch at Legend. Before the mid-1990s China lacked financial professionals who truly understood financial management. Under planned economy, the government allocated resources and capital to all of the state enterprises, and the enterprises were expected to sell the products to assigned customers. The financial manager did not have to plan how to allocate the use of financial resources efficiently and effectively. At the young Legend, sales people were only responsible for product sales, not payments collections. Accountants were only responsible for accounting but did not concern themselves with business performance. Sometimes they found that some payment had not been collected even though the products had been sold for six months already and the sales person who was supposed to be responsible for the transaction had left the country. In 1996 management found that some computers purchased two years previously were still sitting in the warehouse. "The value carried on the books was RMB2,000 but we could only get RMB100 for them," recalled Wang Xiaoyan, an engineer at the time and now Senior Vice President of the Group. "To make our prices more competitive, we had to improve efficiency. This was especially important as the price of components in the computer industry is always very volatile."

Legend was greatly assisted in solving such problems by the introduction of a computerized information system, called Enterprise Resources Planning (ERP) system. The leading role in building this system was played by Gong Guoxing, wife of Chairman Liu and herself a professor and an important Legend executive in its formative years. Since the early 1990s "Madam Gong", as she was known throughout the company, had supervised the company's management information system. She still remembers vividly the difficulties that Legend faced in those days obtaining timely and meaningful operational and accounting information to support decision making. The existing locally developed system could barely meet the needs of a fast-growing company. Many new strategies and policies became almost impossible to implement due to the lack of a decent information system. This state of affairs was not just frustrating; it put Legend at a disadvantage, especially in dealing with foreign competitors.

In early 1997, top management decided to introduce a world-class, full-scale and consistent ERP system. It was not an easy decision to make given the complexity of the company's business and market environment and, above all, the gap between its existing business processes and those standardized processes required by the ERP system. Moreover, no one had much experience in setting up such a system in China. Nevertheless, Liu was determined. "We may fall apart if we go for ERP, but if we do not, we will fall apart while we wait and watch. Legend will not go down, so we have to succeed." Soon a special project team was formed under Madam Gong. A decision was made to choose the German business software provider SAP over other possible vendors. For its part, SAP looked on Legend as a way into the China market. The project began in April 1998. At the time, Legend was in the middle of implementing its own local management resource planning system. Imposing the new system throughout the company meant that the home-made system had to be scrapped. "It was a shame that we had to sacrifice the half-finished system to support the group's overall strategy," recalled Madam Gong. "But it proved to be a good strategy in the long run."

But the most challenging part was yet to come. Madam Gong remembers countless problems that the team encountered during the first two years. The first problem was how to manage the consultants responsible for implementation. The project team turned out to be inefficient. The project manager was replaced several times. Other managers, mostly from Hong Kong, were simply unable to handle the challenge. Issues concerning fee settlement also slowed the process at the initial stage. The consultant team and their counterparts at Legend struggled to work together. Like many other international companies at that time, most of the consultants' work in China had been for the subsidiaries of multinationals. They did not know how to work in a purely Chinese environment. On Legend's side, there were complaints about the training materials not being customized to suit a Chinese company. Too many English terms were not properly explained. Madam Gong had to spend much time and energy simply keeping the lines of communication open.

Another problem was how to bridge the gap between Legend's existing business practices and the "standardized" processes demanded by ERP. Most of these were designed for a Western business environment, which was very different from the one in which Legend had to survive. Legend's project team had to make difficult decisions balancing and reconciling the "China factor" with standard ERP requirements, but ultimately the team, recruited from almost all of the company's business divisions, was up to the task. They were young, eager to learn and spared no effort. Taxis lined up in front of the corporate headquarters in Beijing to take red-eyed team members home after sessions that went on nearly all night. After two years of hard work, the ERP team could finally smile in relief. The system proved a great success, enabling the company to manage different businesses across the country in a more structured and standardized manner than in the past.

Yang also paid close attention to internal management. Every month he held two meetings focusing on logistics, inventory control and cash flow management. "We referred to those meetings as 'to go to court', because Yang was very tough," recalled Wang. "People had to set goals and report on the success of previously stated goals. If they didn't meet the goals by the next meeting, they were heavily criticized and embarrassed." There were two types of "go to court" meetings. In the "small product control meeting", Yang met with the managers from departments like purchasing, planning and sales to review and discuss related matters. In the "big" meeting, Yang met with the managers from all different departments. That meeting focused on reviewing inventory – what and how much was in the warehouse, when they were purchase, at what price – as well as the overall situation. Any and all problems could be brought up, and those who were responsible had to give a thorough explanation and also present solutions for the problems. Those who failed to achieve the goals or solve the problems were rebuked. In addition, Yang also created a department that was fully responsible for payment collection management. Under the new system, sales people were responsible for the status of their accounts. In that way, the collection period on the company's receivables were significantly reduced. This was the last short slat. Within the century and in time for the new millennium he had entirely rebuilt the bucket.

07. The Little Emperors

Having embarked on re-organizing the company. Legend could begin to start thinking about new markets. December 1994, the end of their first year of serious reorganization also marked Legend's tenth anniversary. At the ceremony marking the occasion, Chairman Liu said the company wanted to be making between 500,000 and one million computers a year by 2000. Since they had only shipped 50,000 units in 1994, this seemed to many attending the event to be wildly ambitious. In fact, by 1999 Legend was already shipping one million units.

In the mid-to-late 1990s, the overwhelming market for computers in China was institutional – government ministries and offices, state-owned enterprises, foreign enterprises, universities and the better-off schools. A consumer or home market scarcely existed. That was hardly surprising. In the mid-1990s an ordinary personal computer cost RMB13,000 or more, the equivalent of one or two year's salary for an ordinary family. Moreover, computer technology was very foreign; not only had it come from the United States but most of the operating systems were in English and required skill in using an alphanumeric keyboard. Nevertheless, the reform movement was now nearly two decades old. Living standards, especially in the coastal cities were improving rapidly. A Chinese middle class was emerging; many of whose members were employees of the increasing number of foreign enterprises now laying down roots in China. Students and parents alike admired such white-collar professionals. Skills with computers and foreign languages went hand in hand with good career prospects, and having a computer at home was increasingly seen as strategic to a family's future.

Other factors were working too. Since the early 1980s, China had officially adopted a one-child policy to try to keep its burgeoning population under control and to try to relieve some of the economic pressure on education, employment and housing. Quickly a one-child generation was appearing. This generation was sometimes called the generation of "little emperors" because parents, imbued with the Chinese ethic that places so much emphasis on continuity of family from one generation to the next, doted on them. Spoiled though it might be, this new generation was influencing China's consumption habits. At the same time, China was trying to resurrect its education system, which had been decimated by the Cultural Revolution. Even though China had begun to invest heavily in educational reform, the higher one went in the system, the fewer seats there were. Passing tough examinations was the pathway to better education and thus a better future, better position and better salary. Many parents, who had lost their own dreams in earlier chaotic decades now invested great expectations in their little emperors and empresses and were willing to spend a lot of money on their education, or on instruments, such as computers, that they thought would improve their children's chances. Since it is also Chinese custom that the young look after the old, some of the parents made the investment not just for their children's sake but for their own as well. Whatever the reason, educating the little emperor had become a family priority and computers were suddenly on every family's shopping list.

Legend was quick to exploit the emergence of a home market for computers. The idea of a "Home PC" for the Chinese family was first proposed by a Legend subsidiary, Legend Jiao Yu Dianzi Co. Ltd., whose name translates as "Legend Educational Electronics". The early design was based on the then low-end 286PC. In order to make the machine affordable to Chinese households; the Home PC was very simply equipped. One model, priced at RMB3,000, didn't even have a hard disk. Yang Yuanqing merged Jiao Yu Dianzi with his own PC unit and decided to begin upgrading the machine. In 1995 Legend rolled out a completely different and smart-looking Home PC, with strong multimedia functions and a 486 central processing unit. The computer, among its other features, had a television card to receive TV signals. Legend recognized that these customers were different from their usual official and corporate customers. They could not be assumed to have any computer knowledge at all. Legend set up training classes, where many of the students were whole families ~ parents and their teenage children. They started with the basics, such as where to place ones fingers on the keyboard. "I had to go on radio and even television to do hotline call-in programs where people could ask questions about PCs," recalled Wang Xiaoyan, in charge of post-sales training at that time. "We promoted a campaign named 'Legend Computer Express', which went into schools and organizations, cities and small towns, to give demonstrations and show off the computers, letting people touch them."

During the introduction of the Home PC, Legend had failures as well as successes. For example, the TV chip was imported and not strong enough to receive China's rather weak signals, giving unclear pictures. Besides, there was not enough room on the motherboard to insert the TV card. But through trial and error Legend gradually developed a sense for what the home consumer wanted and needed in a computer and cultivated its ability to satisfy those wants and needs. This led to a distinction being made between what Legend called the "Function PC" and the "Application PC". In the West, consumers tend to buy the basic computer and then add optional devices and software to suit their needs, studying themselves how to install the components and the software. Realizing that the Chinese consumer needed a lot more hand-holding, Legend strove to provide a PC equipped with all of the desired functions, including hardware, software and service. This was the "Function PC". Then realizing that most families purchased computers to further educate their children, it developed the "Happy Family" series software, which included programs on basic computer knowledge, educational tutorials, games, home finance and affairs management. This series shaped the "Application PC". Taking the concept further, Legend developed "application" computers and software which targeted directly the special needs of small and medium-sized businesses, tax collection bureaus and schools. An "e-classroom" model linked a teacher's computer to dozens of student's terminals.

Legend based its initial success mainly on distribution, training and after sales service. Still the company's research and development team made numerous innovations in its formative years. During this time Legend's Hong Kong research and development team designed two new ASIC chips and more than 50 models of motherboards and add-on products. Legend add-on cards included Chinese laser printer cards and various multi-function input/output cards. The research and development team made it possible for Legend to use the latest technology in designing PCs that took advantage of its in-depth understanding of its Chinese customers' needs. Starting from 1994, to further enhance product development capability, Yang established a product planning department to link R&D, marketing and sales. The purpose was to establish a close connection between new technology development and the market. Legend has continued to strengthen its research and development activities, both by recruiting new scientific talent and establishing cooperation with foreign companies such as Microsoft and Intel, merging their advanced technologies into

Legend products at an early stage. The lesson of the little emperors is that China is a fast-growing and demanding society whose market for computer technology is huge and increasingly sophisticated. It will be some time before the winnowing stops. Meanwhile, only the fittest will survive.

08. Going Public

In late 1993, a thick prospectus arrived on the desks of many Hong Kong financial advisors, announcing that Legend Holdings Ltd. was planning to raise HK$224,437,500 on the stock market. Ten years after being founded in a decrepit two-room office as the offshoot of a national government research institute, Legend – at least the Hong Kong side of it – was going public. Stock market analysts were optimistic about the pending issue, predicting that Legend could become one of the bigger "China plays", outperforming even Stone Electronic Technology, which had been successfully floated the previous August. "With more than 50 percent of sales coming from across the border, Legend is exploiting China's burgeoning demand for computers as the country moves towards computerization amid fast-paced economic growth," intoned the *South China Morning Post*. Noting that the new issue was being offered at a fairly conservative 10.7 times prospective earnings; it was deemed a "bargain". The investors went on to note that Legend had become the leading distributor of foreign-branded computers in China and that Legend Beijing had also carved out a niche with its own Legend computers, just behind Great Wall among the domestic brands. They praised the group's strong management, relatively high brand recognition in China and "prospects of increasing application of computers in the country". But they also worried about prospects for profits. China's economy was still in transition to a market economy and the computer industry remained highly competitive and characterized by rapid technological development.

Legend's stock issue went on sale on February 14, 1994. The new issue was oversubscribed 405 times, proving optimists correct while giving the company temporary possession of HK$83 billion, about US$10 billion, until refund checks to unsuccessful bidders were dispatched. Legend was still left with a total of HK$217 million (about US$28 million) from the sale of 168,750,000 shares issued at HK$1.33 per share. On the first day of trading, Legend's share price reached a high of HK$2.07 before closing at HK$2.00. This increase of nearly 50 per cent in the value of the shares was all the more remarkable in that the Hong Kong stock market index actually declined on that day. Of the proceeds, the directors stated that they planned to spend approximately HK$60 million (about US$7.7 million) to finance additional overseas sales offices in Europe, Australia and North America; approximately HK$70 million (about US$9 million) to expand and develop production and R&D capabilities, and the balance to bolster working capital.

Sales of Legend-brand computers had begun to take off in 1994 and by 1996 Legend was firmly established itself in the Chinese market. Profits at Legend Beijing also began to soar, rising from RMB12.9 million in fiscal year 1994/95 to RMB22.6 million in fiscal year 1995/96 to RMB85 million in fiscal year 1996/97 (an increase of 123 per cent – profits would go to RMB189 million in fiscal 1997/98). However, during this period Legend Hong Kong, led by the local management team, was losing money. In one year Legend Holdings (HK) went from a profit of HK$86 million to a net loss in 1996 of HK$195 million. As the analysts had predicted, the industry was volatile and subject to fluctuations in price. The year 1995 in particular had proved challenging for the entire industry. Fueled by the industry growth in 1994 and the advent of many new and exciting technologies, companies rushed into expanding capacity and new plants. By the end of 1995, the oversupply had triggered a price war that caused the prices of personal computers to fall dramatically. Due to faulty analysis of the market, the company had overstocked inventory. The collapse of component prices seriously also affected Legend's motherboard business. At the same time the company's distribution of AST products suffered from internal problems with the American firm.

These problems took their toll on Legend Hong Kong's share price. From a post-listing high above HK$2.00 the share price had fallen to HK$0.32. To address this problem, Chairman Liu decided to inject the assets of Legend Beijing into Legend Holdings (Hong Kong). He felt that the merger between Legend Hong Kong and Legend Beijing would create a new business synergy, allowing the group to increase profits and become the leading high-tech stock on the Hong Kong stock exchange. The asset injection would give Legend shareholders a better chance to profit from the rapid growth of the computer market in China. Technically, this was to be accomplished by having the Hong Kong branch purchase controlling shares of three major businesses: the Legend-brand PC; the foreign brand distribution business and the systems integration business. To pay for this, the listed company would issue 879 million new shares at HK$2.38 in November 1997. Getting the merger approved was complicated. The sale had to be approved by both the China Securities Regulatory Commission and, because Legend was actually selling state-owned property, by the State Asset Management Bureau. The latter was used to valuing huge state-enterprises worth billions. By their standards, Legend seemed woefully undervalued. Legend had net assets valued at HK$171 million (about US$22 million) and projected earnings of no less than HK$155 million (about US$20 million), which were being sold for 13.5 times earnings, or about HK$2 billion (about US$256 million), a 13.5 profit to equity ratio. "They could not understand why foreign investors would pay $2 billion for HK$140 million in assets," recalled Mary Ma, Chief Financial Officer of Legend. "They were comparing us to an iron and steel works, for example, that had RMB40 billion worth of assets but was listed for only a few million because of low earnings."

It was a propitious time to go on the market. Hong Kong was in the middle of its "red chip" frenzy. "Anything connected with China looked attractive," said Ma. "Some companies wanted to rename their company the 'China Something Company,' just so they could cash in. Everybody was looking for some kind of asset from their Chinese parent that they could 'inject' into the locally listed company." Every new issue was over subscribed by many times, and the stock price usually shot up in the days immediately following. Although Legend rode this bubble, its intent was different. While some other companies were just looking for something Chinese to turn into a "red chip". Legend's purpose was to unify and focus its business under higher quality management and to otherwise take advantage of the synergies achieved by bringing Beijing and Hong Kong operations under one roof.

The merger took place in November 1997. With the reorganization, the new Legend Group's stock took off, becoming one of the biggest counters on the Hong Kong bourse. The share price rose from a low of 29 cents a share in February 1997 to a high of HK$70 in 2000, when it split four to one. In Liu's view, going public had two major effects on Legend's future. One, of course, was raising needed capital. The other was learning to deal with shareholders. "The purpose of going public is not entirely to raise the money. Dealing with shareholders is a way to improve performance because shareholders demand transparency and systematic management."

In 1984, Legend was born in this small bungalow in Beijing, China.

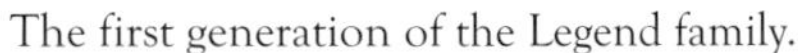

The first generation of the Legend family.

The second generation of the Legend family.

Legend Hong Kong was formally established in 1988.

In 1994, 10 years after its establishment, Legend was listed on the Hong Kong Stock Exchange. It became one of the constituent stocks of the Hang Seng Index in 2000.

In 1994, Legend set up the Legend Science and Technology Park in Huiyang, Guangdong Province in southern China, its first manufacturing base.

People are Legend's most precious assets.

Passing the torch. In April 2001, Chairman Liu turned the entire Legend operations over to Yang Yuanqing.

The official spin-off of Digital China from Legend Group in 2001.

China's top government leaders including Hu Jintao and Jiang Zemin have visited Legend.

Eye on the world, Legend has formed strategic alliances
with leading international partners.

In July 2003, under the lead of The Science and Technology Department of the Ministry of Information Industry, Legend and four other enterprises formed the "Intelligent Grouping and Resources Sharing Standardization Working Group" to work towards the industry standards development of information technology in China.

In August 2003, Legend, together with Intel, announced the establishment of the "Intel-Lenovo Technology Advancement Center".

In April 2003, the Group officially launched its new logo "lenovo", in preparation for its international expansion.

Lenovo became the first Chinese enterprise to join the International Olympic Committee's worldwide sponsorship programme on March 26, 2004.

Chairman Liu Chuanzhi (right) and CEO Yang Yuanqing (left)

The young and energetic management team, under the leadership of Yang Yuanqing, in front of Legend's headquarters in Beijing.

A PC production line

Legend's office in Shenzhen, Southern China.

The Group's manufacturing base in Huiyang, Guangdong Province, Southern China.

The Group's automated warehouse, supported by advanced ERP system.

Legend's 1+1 Home PC Specialty Shops provide customers with face-to-face direct sales of Legend IT products and services.

Legend's corporate IT shops provide corporate customers with a full range of IT solutions.

Legend Sunshine Services allows customers to experience hassle-free and convenient after-sales services.

Apart from PCs, Legend is also entering into the mobile handset market in China.

Legend's products satisfy every possible need of different members in the digital era.

A Legend advertisement billboard at Zhongguancun in Beijing, which is known as China's Silicon Valley.

09. Seek Truth from Facts

Systematic management had been a Legend preoccupation from the beginning but the group was also showing that it could be creative. Still, raising money was one thing; using it well was another. About the same time it had first gone to the Hong Kong stock market in 1994, Legend had begun an initial investment of RMB800 million in the Legend Science and Technology Park in Huiyang, a small city in the Pearl River basin of Guangdong Province not far from Hong Kong to serve as its export manufacturing base. Shenzhen had become more of a financial center than a manufacturing base. Dongguan, a popular location for many Hong Kong manufacturers, offered better conditions but could not fulfill Legend's need for space. Although somewhat remote, Huiyang had land. Legend would eventually acquire some 800,000 square meters there.

But how would the Technology Park be used? Legend had previously determined that its must sell abroad but had remained undecided whether to use the facilities at Huiyang primarily to manufacture products for other companies, especially foreign companies, or to make and sell its own branded products. In 1998 Chairman Liu and several other senior executives took an exploratory trip to Taiwan. During that trip they visited all of Taiwan's major technology enterprises, including the most famous Taiwan IT company Acer. They returned having learned an important difference between their situation and those of Taiwan's manufacturers. Taiwan enterprises mostly did contract manufacturing for other companies because the local market was too small for them to establish their own brands and establishing an international brand without the support of a strong domestic market was very difficult. Comparative advantage lay in working for others. The American giant IBM, for example, did not manufacture personal computers itself; it outsourced the work to a Taiwanese contract manufacturer. For most Taiwanese enterprises, contract manufacturing was the only way to survive. Acer was the only Taiwanese company determined to build its own brand in the international market. But building a brand internationally had proven difficult; in particular, Acer had few successes in the U.S. Legend's situation was different. Unlike Taiwan, the mainland China market on its own was already big enough to sustain a brand. Legend's advantage was staring it right in the face.

The trip caused Legend to re-evaluate its strategy. Its management came back more committed than ever to focus on the China market. Developing international markets would have to wait. Guo Wei, later to become the president of the Legend spin-off Digital China, was dispatched from the Beijing office to oversee the development of the Huiyang base. He faced several challenges. It was difficult to acquire talent; Huiyang was remote, transportation was inconvenient and living conditions were fairly primitive. Workers from Beijing did not want to move there. Guangdong province was notorious for cut-throat management practices. Managers, many representing absentee owners in Hong Kong or Taiwan, had a reputation for caring little about the welfare of their employees. Guo and his colleagues believed that much of its success had come from a different approach, from incorporating the aspirations of its staff into the development of the enterprise. Legend's managers had gotten the chance to become owners through stock option plans unknown to other Chinese companies. Now they offered incentives to employees, including job relocation and training. Collecting and nurturing the needed talent at the Technology Park was a long process, but in the end rewarding. It paid off in staff loyalty. When there was a fire on a hill opposite the Technology Park, the workers in the other factories nearby didn't care. Legend's workers put down their tools and helped to put out the fire. Step by step, the Huiyang base was built.

The initial plan had been to use Huiyang as the base for developing a large-scale, export-oriented contract manufacturing business. There were to be five plants, for the making of PC monitors, printed circuit boards, CD-ROM assembly lines and so forth. At the same time a research team was to be established in Shenzhen. Creating a research center would in turn help solve the problems of recruiting talented engineers. But after the reconnaissance mission to Taiwan in 1998 these plans changed. Development of the Technology Park was linked with building the branded business of the listed company. By 2001 the park produced RMB2.8 billion worth of products, mostly personal computers, motherboards and printed circuit boards. As of 2003, about 280,000 square meters of the Huiyang space had been developed into factories, office buildings and dormitories for a Legend staff that had come to number some 4,000. Chinese enterprises, especially state-owned enterprises, do not easily change strategies. Many companies during the reform period had lost opportunities because they were not able to "seek truth from facts" and then act on their insights. Legend was, and stands out in this respect.

10. Legend Strikes Back

1996 was to be Legend's year of reckoning, the year when all of the reengineering, the cost-cutting, the re-ordering of the distribution, inventory and cash management systems, the successful public listing, all of the changes of the previous three years were to pay off. By 1996, too, Legend had increased its manufacturing capability to about 500,000 computers a year, giving it the volume to take advantage of any increase in sales. The Legend brand PC business consecutively achieved annual growth rate of over 100% in turnover in 1996 and 1997. In 1997, Legend brand PC became the best selling brand in China, with a market share of 10.7%. For the very first time, a local computer brand had surpassed the major international brands in the China PC market.

Legend continued to increase sales and by 1999 had captured 20.1 percent of the market ~ by 2000, 26.3 percent. Since then Legend has never surrendered the leading position. It would be easy to dismiss Legend's success as selling cheap products made from cheap labor. It is true that Legend enjoyed lower costs for components made in China, but that is only one part of the story. To win the PC war, Legend followed two main strategies: to be there faster and cheaper than foreign competitors and to tailor its products to meet local needs. In the early 1990s, foreign manufacturers were selling mainly their second line computers in China. In other words, PC makers were selling 486PCs at the same time they were introducing models with the powerful new Pentium microprocessors to their more discerning customers in the West. China was becoming a dumping ground for outdated computers at outdated prices. Legend saw the opportunity. It struck up a partnership with Intel and began manufacturing Pentium-based desktops for the China market. Component prices were falling rapidly but Yang Yuanqing's work to streamline the management of inventory now had the company prepared. Legend was able to take immediate advantage by lowering the price of its computers. Meanwhile, with rising production, the company was continuing to benefit from greater and greater economies of scale. Legend cut the price of a Pentium-based PC to the equivalent of US$1,200 yet was still able to maintain margins.

Yang described the pivotal meeting that was a turning point in the history of the Chinese PC market:

> "On March 5, 1996, we had a meeting with Intel about what to do. Legend's scale was still not sufficient to significantly reduce prices. Our options were between continuing to sell the 486PC or switching to Pentium. I wanted to try to sell a Pentium PC for RMB10,000, but some of the attendees in the meeting did not agree with the idea of selling high-products for low prices. They thought it would be too risky. My idea was to work very fast and efficiently while cutting costs and taking advantage of dropping component prices. I wanted to expand and take advantage of economies of scale. We were not sure it would work, but the others reluctantly agreed. After one month, our sales doubled."

When one campaign was completed, they immediately launched another. They ran a campaign for a 75 megahertz PC, then 100 MHz and then 135. "Because we had such good inventory control, we could work faster than our competitors. When Intel rolled out a new chip, we had no significant old-model inventory to sell. We could introduce a new model immediately," recalled Yang.

Competitors, particularly foreign companies, underestimated Legend's strategy and strength and failed to follow suit with lower prices. Said Yang, "We didn't give them a break. They were far away and couldn't follow us fast enough. All the eyes of the world turned to watch Legend as we set the market. They were no longer watching the foreign firms." Many foreign companies assumed that Legend's prices were too low and that the company would lose money and go under. But actually profits increased by 200 percent. "The first time we became number one in the Chinese PC market, foreigners thought it was just luck," said Liu. "It was not easy for them to understand why they lost the game."

Legend was not the only winner in the PC wars. The Chinese consumer also won, since foreign firms could no longer dump second-class products into the China market. If they wanted a place at the table, they had to offer the most advanced technology. The industry as a whole also won, since better products at better prices brought more buyers into the market; the pie got bigger for everyone, about 20 percent bigger. Other local computer brands, that had virtually disappeared in the disastrous year of 1993, such as Founder, Stone and Great Wall, made a comeback. Local news media acted as a cheering squad and encouraged the public to "Buy Chinese". Legend's successes and its constant media attention gradually changed the perception of Chinese consumers that foreign products were more reliable and of a higher quality.

Despite the success of its own brand, Legend's distribution of foreign brand computers remained an important part of its business. By 1997, its network had grown to some 3,000 distributors, selling such brands as Hewlett-Packard, Toshiba and Sun. Distribution still accounted for 31 percent of total revenues. Legend had weathered the storm. It had survived the battering of 1993 and come back to command the market in 1996. By now it was already beginning to think of itself as a future Fortune 500 Company, perhaps the first Chinese enterprise to make that August listing. But another challenge loomed, the growth of the Internet.

Part 3

New Directions

11. The Challenge of The Internet

With its huge population, China stepped into the new millennium with the potential to become the largest Internet market in the world. Internet penetration was increasing rapidly, if from a low base. Growth of the Internet market saw the emergence of many new Chinese-language "dotcoms", including ones that would emerge as market leaders, such as China.com, Sina.com and Sohu.com. Initially, Legend stayed on the sidelines, but in 1999 when it decided to enter the Internet market it did so with a clear vision. That strategy was, firstly, to use Internet access to drive the sale of hardware, including PCs and other new products and, secondly, to use its commanding position in the PC market to dominate the Internet itself.

Legend's first move in this new game was to develop a new personal computer called the Tianxi (also known as the Conet PC). This machine was equipped with the latest Pentium III microprocessor, 56k modem and even a DVD player. But the really revolutionary feature was its "one-touch-to-the-Net" feature, which enabled users to connect with the Internet simply by pushing a button. Through a special arrangement with China Telecom Ltd., the country's largest telecommunications company, buyers of the Tianxi PC also received a year of free Internet access. Special keys took users to popular sites, e-mail and technical support menus. A digital pen allowed them to write Chinese-character e-mails. "We thought the hardware design for the idea of a 'one-touch-to-the-Net' system was possible, but we had a hard time trying to figure out how users could connect using the same button in different regions," said Jia Zhaohui, the leader of the Tianxi research team. Working closely with China Telecom, Jia and his team managed to design a system that allowed nationwide roaming. This had simplified the Internet registration process dramatically, enabling users to gain easy access and enjoy the fun of net surfing. The Tianxi (Conet PC) quickly became the most popular PC in China, selling more than 200,000 units in the first six months.

Tailoring its products to meet local needs had given Legend an advantage that was difficult for competitors to match. Liu stated later that, "American manufacturers have more advanced technology, but their products have to serve the world market. Legend's strength comes from its ability to develop features tailored to the unique needs of the Chinese market." The Tianxi system was hard for competitors to copy because the user's telecom account came built into the computer. That way the consumer didn't need to go to the telecom office to get an account, something that was still very complicated to do in China. This was made possible only because of close cooperation with China Telecom and its nationwide network. Each province in China has its own telecom office. Legend needed to make agreements with 30 branches in order to make the computer truly national. Jia noted that working out these problems required the efforts of more than 100 engineers and an investment of $1.2 million. The machine itself has some 40 patents. But the investment quickly paid off. Within six months, Legend had earned a net profit of $3 million from Tianxi sales.

The next move was to develop a line of new products, such as workstations, servers, palm-sized computers and notebook computers all designed for the Chinese-language Internet. Through cooperation with China Telecom, users could access the Internet in some 2,000 towns and cities throughout the country, making them truly portable.

This meant that people traveling among different cities no longer needed to apply for a local log-in account. They simply dialed up the local telecom network, using the same dial-up number no matter which city they were in. This not only simplified the connection process but also saved on long-distance charges. As with the Tianxi, a Legend notebook or palm computer user was entitled to a period of free Internet access. Legend also decided to produce and sell set-top boxes that allowed people to surf the Net with their TV sets. Costing the equivalent of about US$400 and using Venus software from Microsoft, the box allowed users to do online trading and to access market trends and company data. This device brought the Internet within reach of consumers who had not been able to pay the US$1,900-equivalent cost of a Tianxi computer.

Legend's next move was to bundle the Tianxi – and notebook computers and other Internet connectors – with its own web portal. Rather than trying to hook up with other existing Chinese-language portals, such as China.com, Legend decided to go it alone. In April 2000 it introduced its own comprehensive site, called FM365. The name derived from the user interface, which looked like a radio dial, and projected the company's confidence that subscribers would want to use it 365 days of the year. The company planned to invest about HK$200 million (about US$25.6 million) in the venture. It signed cooperative agreements with nearly 200 content and technical providers, and planned to recruit experienced professionals to run the portal. The portal would include information channels covering such topics as news, education, entertainment, stocks and shopping. There would also be a "Virtual Community" for e-mails and chat rooms, search engines and e-commerce. "Our goal is to establish FM365 as one of the largest portals in China with some 8 million page views a day," Liu told the media at the time of the launch.

Revenues would come mainly from advertising and on-line trading commissions.

Together with the Internet boom came the popularity of the Pocket PC. Taiwan producers of mobile PCs had claimed Legend couldn't make its own without help from the Americans. Taking up their challenge, Liu put his engineers to work. By the later part of 1998, they had produced the first Chinese-designed palm computer. In November 2000, Legend simultaneously launched three new Internet-connected palm personal computers and a special Web portal for palm PCs called Palm365.com. All became part of the new "Tianji" series. The Tianji 5000, with a full color screen, was the first palm PC in China to use a Microsoft operating system. It offered users a "pocket office", with web browsing and e-mail. The Tianji 820e came installed with a Palm365.com e-mail account, and the "Tianji Stock" function enabled the user to receive and process enormous amounts of information from the Shanghai and Shenzhen stock exchanges. The new Palm365.com portal especially designed for mobile palm PCs, allowed users to access their e-mail accounts through a single address.

Legend would continue to produce advanced models in the series. The Tianji XP100, which used a Microsoft operating system and Intel microprocessors, was the first pocket PC in China with multimedia functions, allowing its users to play songs and Flash video. "Internet services and products have tremendous market potential," said Yang Yuanqing. "Building on Legend's technology and brand name and cooperating with international and local partners, Legend is promoting the rapid development of Internet service in China." To promote its Internet services, Legend launched a large-scale promotional campaign: "Legend's Internet Journey in the PRC." The promotional campaign brought Legend computer products and Internet applications to more than 300 small and medium cities and greatly boosted computer sales. Legend's top managers also visited these cities and participated in many seminars and exhibitions. Throughout the campaign, Legend established relationships with local governments and clients to gain a better understanding of user needs.

Thus Legend's plan for exploiting the advantages of the Internet developed rapidly from 1998 to 2000. The fundamental strategy was to take advantage of the synergies between Legend's PC business and the Internet, letting the two sides of the business complement and reinforce each other. The growing interest in the Net would obviously boost sales of computers and the profits from these sales would help subsidize the development of Internet services. What goes up rapidly can crash easily. The global Internet bubble would not last but before it burst Legend would manage to float itself into a new paradigm of business. It was becoming a multidimensional company fully engaged in the digital revolution changing Chinese society and the global community it now so eagerly embraced.

12. Strategic Partners

Legend's involvement with the Internet went hand in hand with its own more profound connections with the outside world, inevitable despite its decision to focus on the burgeoning China market. Almost from the very beginning, Legend had forged profitable arrangements with American manufacturers, distributing computers and printers for Hewlett-Packard, IBM, AST and others. Many relationships had been enduring – the one with HP having lasted for 14 years. But as its product range grew and its own technological sophistication developed, it found itself dealing with the giants even more. The "legends" of the computer world were beginning to take notice of this "Legend in the making" in China. Moreover, as the overseas market for personal computers was clearly slowing, many of these companies were anxious to do more business in China. Once happy enough to let Legend distribute their products, they were now more open to technological cooperation.

The principle Legend followed in forging deeper cooperation with foreign companies was "ally two strengths". In other words, it looked for partners with strengths that complemented its own. As its own strengths grew, so did the list of world leading technology companies with which it deepened its relationships: IBM, HP, Intel, Microsoft, Hitachi, Siemens, Texas Instruments and AOL, etc. The relationship with Intel has been especially significant for both partners. One of the reasons that Legend succeeded in capturing the largest share of the Chinese computer market in 1996 was its decision to use only the best of Intel's microprocessors, the then new Pentium chips that fell steadily in price just as Legend's market share was taking off.

For its part, Intel had recognized Legend's potential when it was still a very small company and provided significant support and guidance. By 1995, Intel had already selected Legend as its first "strategic partner" in China. Such a partnership suited Intel's plans to enter the Chinese market. Intel's Pentium III chips and Legend's Pentium III computers were introduced simultaneously and both companies benefited from Legend's increasing success with the Internet PCs.

In addition to this basic commercial relationship, Intel actively promoted Legend's development as a corporation, providing it with opportunities to learn advanced management techniques. Most of Legend's executives have participated in Intel's organizational training programs. Meanwhile, Legend's growing success in the China market has provided Intel with a cushion against periodic fluctuations in the Western high-tech market. The relationship has been enduring. In March of 2002, for example, Legend announced that it had become one of Intel's eight global partners in promoting the Xeon Server. Legend and Intel will jointly promote the Pentium IV single-processor server; meanwhile, Intel is helping Legend towards its goal to become the premier server manufacturer in China.

As Legend has broadened its focus beyond PCs into services and related technology-driven businesses, it has needed even more partners. For example, seeing the convergence of data and voice technology and the resultant growth in market potential for mobile telephony, Legend decided to begin making mobile telephone handsets. It launched a joint venture with Xiamen Overseas Chinese Electronic Co. Ltd. (Xoceco) to research, produce and sell handsets in February 2002. To research the latest wireless technology, Legend teamed up with Texas Instruments, jointly establishing a digital signal-processing laboratory in Beijing. TI's wireless chipset has captured 60 percent of the wireless products in the world, including such famous brands as Nokia. The decision to jointly explore short distance wireless technology with Texas Instruments should enhance Legend's competitiveness in this field.

13. From Red Chip to Blue Chip

To meet the capital needs of a growing business, Legend went back to the Hong Kong stock market in March 2000, successfully placing 50 million new shares and raising HK$1,651 million (about US$212 million). It was not the first time that Legend had raised capital through issuing shares. It had successfully gone to the investing public in 1994 and again in the middle of the "red chip" frenzy of 1997. But Legend was now becoming a bigger player, its market symbol – "992" – having become one of the hottest counters on the Hong Kong bourse. The introduction of the Tianxi (Conet) Internet PC in 1999 was one of the most significant technology stories of the year, and one not lost on potential investors. The growth of its business had also generated lots of media coverage and increased awareness of Legend overseas. The company was selected as one of the "Ten Hot Global High-Tech Company" stocks by the American business magazine *Fortune*. Other stories focused on the number of people who were getting rich on the Legend stock. One woman said she had bought two million shares at 30 cents in 1996 and sold at HK$20.00 in late 1999.

But Legend was finding that its new prominence was bringing with it new responsibilities. When Legend was first listed, the managers thought the only goal was to raise money. They knew next to nothing about transparency or the other rules and responsibilities that come with being a public company. For example, when in 1997 Legend decided to merge its assets in Beijing and Hong Kong through a stock acquisition, Chairman Liu proudly informed mainland newspapers of the impending move, not knowing that this violated the stock trading rules. The next day trading in "992" was suspended for two days as a punishment. This occurred several times and Liu learned the hard way: he had to be careful what he said in public. The first time Liu took a roadshow to Europe, he was surprised that he was not greeted with the same warm treatment he was accustomed to in China. He was asked all kinds of tough questions. At first, Liu felt wronged; later he came to understand that he had a new kind of "boss". "Before I had only one boss, but CAS (Chinese Academy of Sciences) never asked me anything. I relied on my own initiative to do things. We began to think about issues of credibility. Legend began to learn how to become a truly international company."

Meanwhile, the red chip bubble had burst. The frenzy of 1997 was succeeded in 1998 by a year of scandals in some of the newly listed Chinese companies and the investing public had turned against the lot. The situation for high-tech-related red chips was even worse. Liu knew that his company had to improve its image with investors if it was not to be tarred with the broad brush of discrimination against all new China counters. These days Legend is acknowledged throughout the global investment community for the transparency of its operations and the effectiveness of its investor relations work. It has received numerous accolades from the international financial press, such as "Best Asia-Pacific Company Investor Relations in the UK Market," (*UK IR Magazine*), "Overall Best Managed Company in China" (*Asiamoney*) and "Best in Commitment to Shareholder Value" (*FinanceAsia*). In August 2000, Legend's stock became one of the constituents of the Hang Seng Index of the Hong Kong Stock Exchange and several other indices. Legend is now recognized as one of new mainland-based companies in the listing that places high priority on investor relationship in its overall management. "Nowadays, Chinese companies are just beginning to deal with issues of credibility that Legend learned earlier," Liu reflected.

The primary responsibility for developing Legend's investor relations team fell to Mary Ma, the company's chief financial officer since 1990. Under Ma's supervision, Legend's investor relations staff successfully molded the Western point of view into Legend's corporate culture by making themselves the main bridge between the company's very Chinese management hierarchy and the international community. Here is how Ma describes their approach:

> "Between the board and shareholders the first thing we emphasize is transparency. Especially with minority shareholders, we disclose everything, whether it is good or bad, the positive and the negative, the risks. Second, we deliver; we never say any empty words to them. Also important is the relationship between the board of directors and the major shareholder, which is different from most foreign companies. Companies such as IBM don't have a majority shareholder. Everyone is in the minority. We have a majority holder. And if it doesn't behave properly, it could jeopardize the whole thing. Fortunately, our major shareholder is very supportive."

Like other elements of Legend's management, the investor relations team was run by a small group of young professionals, all skillful, rational and visionary. Their mission was two-fold: not only did they have to present a clear picture of Legend and its evolving business to investors and keep Legend in the market's eye, they had to build its credibility. For any Chinese enterprise, the concept of maximizing investor's return was still pretty foreign. Through its proactive investor relations approach, Legend earned a reputation for being the most transparent of the mainland's red chip companies. All major issues related to such matters as appointment of board members, major share transfers, mergers and acquisitions were disclosed fairly and equally. While firms listed on the Hong Kong exchange are required to report their results only twice a year, Legend followed the Western practice of issuing quarterly reports. Four times a year, the board reviewed performance results and plans. Then the audit committee, made up of independent directors representing the minority shareholders, reviewed the financial results. A remuneration committee headed by independent non-executive director representing the majority shareholder monitors management salaries. The chief financial officer routinely provided detailed breakdowns for financial analysts. Said a top executive of one major investment bank in Hong Kong in *Fortune*: "From a governance and transparency standpoint, they are head and shoulders above any other Chinese company. There is no one really close."

Legend goes on the road twice a year to meet with institutional investors all over the world. Each roadshow usually involves some 70 to 80 meetings. Mary Ma normally does about eight meetings a day. Legend visits three countries in Europe, then moves to the U.S. and returns via Singapore and Japan. Legend also has an e-mail system to communicate with institutional investors. Additionally it participates in investment conferences five or six times a year and invites more than a thousand investors a year to visit Legend manufacturing and research operations in Shanghai and Shenzhen, and its office in Hong Kong.

In March 2002, Legend and China Central Television (CCTV) co-hosted the first ever investor relations conference held in Beijing. Liu and Ma gave two separate speeches to share Legend's corporate governance philosophy with regulators, scholars and the media.

Everywhere officers echoed the CEO Yang's philosophy. "We're not looking for short-term profits; our ultimate goal is to become a vibrant and long-lasting enterprise." At such presentations Mary Ma spent a lot of time describing the unusual circumstances of being a "state-owned, privately-run" business in China today. "The very concept of corporate governance in China is embryonic, and society lacks an understanding of it. Oversight is still relatively weak because the government and supervisory agencies need more clearly defined laws and regulations," she points out. In China's state sector, the state is still the biggest shareholder, essentially the majority shareholder, controlling more than 60 per cent in most state enterprises, the board members and managers are appointed by the government, resulting in frequent intervention. And there is little incentive for management or checks and balances. One result is minority shareholder interests cannot be effectively protected. The atmosphere had become different at Legend, where a clearly defined ownership structure supports transparency. Successive stock offering had reduced the state's ownership from 73 percent in 1997 to about 57 percent in 2002; the stake of public investors and staff had risen to 43 percent.

The issuance of new shares by the listed company allowed more global investors to hold Legend's stock and allowed Legend to have more capital for reinvestment. It also marked the beginning of another stage in the company's development. By the turn of the new millennium, Legend had grown through a difficult childhood, survived its adolescent troubles and weathered the ups and downs of young adulthood. It was now functioning as a mature, successful corporate player, recognized as such in the international community and increasingly ready to face the challenges of a new century.

Part 4

Passing the Torch

14. The Issue of Ownership

By the turn of the millennium China had moved a long way on its path toward a market economy, but left largely unresolved was the issue of ownership. This presented a major problem for Legend as it grew, since it provided neither the "iron rice bowl" security of a traditional state-owned enterprise nor the incentives of a capitalist corporation. Until Legend went public in 1994, it was totally owned by the Chinese Academy of Sciences (CAS). As the head of a "state-owned, privately-run" corporation, Liu had almost unlimited freedom to run the company in the best way he saw fit, but he had few tools with which to reward the people who had left the security of state research institutes, universities or enterprises to join his venture. As seen with his early move to Hong Kong, he could not even pay competitive wages. A large portion of an employee's formal salary was diverted back to the state. In this respect, Legend was no different from hundreds of other technology firms set up on Electric Street in the early 1980s. Indeed, Legend was at a disadvantage in attracting talent since it was not perceived as being one of the more favored "national champion" enterprises operating under state protection.

Liu recognized the importance of motivation early and did what he could to address it. Of course, he had already seen what had helped propel development of technology enterprises in the West. "When Microsoft's Bill Gates and Intel's Andrew Grove started their companies, their initial capital was even less than the RMB200,000 given to Legend. Had it not been for the strong tie between the companies' performance and the managers' expectations of future personal wealth, these two companies would not have been so successful today," said Liu. He was also aware that Legend's rapid expansion in recent years was due to the recruitment of capable young managers in key positions. This would not have happened if Liu had not been able to persuade the first generation of scientist-managers to make way for a younger leadership. And this would not have happened had the older generation not had something to look forward to in retirement. In most state-owned firms, scientists and managers were paid low wages, and their living standards dropped even more when they retired. Hence they had little incentive to groom younger talent before stepping aside to let them take over.

Liu has always believed that he was accountable not only to the corporation but also to the society. He continuously tried to instill proper values within his younger employees. In China, people born in the 1930s and 1940s did not develop a strong desire to get rich. They had grown up uneasy with the concept of dedicating one's life to making money. Instead, they had focused more on sharing in and contributing to society – values fundamental to the success of China's Communist-led revolution of 1949. But, the extremes of the Cultural Revolution in the 1960s and 1970s caused disillusionment and later the opening to the West brought into China conflicting values. The inadequacies of the social welfare system also meant that people worried a lot about an impoverished old age and thus clung tenaciously to any job they might have. Some people even made money in immoral or illegal ways and went unpunished because the legal system in the country was not very well developed. Liu continually emphasized that Legend employees must be self-disciplined and socially responsible. He often cited the example of the Hongkong and Shanghai Banking Corporation, which had similarly demanded a higher standard of its employees during a time in the 1950s and early 1960s when corruption was rife in the British colony. He wanted Legend to set a similar example in China. He set the tone by punishing those who were dishonest or corrupt. He even helped to send a few who broke the law to jail, albeit rehiring some of them after they got out.

Liu encouraged and did his best to help those employees who wanted to study to improve. But the problem of how to reward employees materially and encourage ability in a society where everyone was theoretically equal occupied Liu for many years. From the very beginning, Liu paid attention to improving the incentive scheme. At first he offered bonuses. But this was already a fairly common practice in China, and the bonuses were usually distributed equally, without any reference to an employee's performance. Then in 1992 he made a proposal to the Chinese Academy of Sciences (CAS) that was almost revolutionary. At that time CAS owned 100 percent of Legend. In theory as well as law, it was thus entitled to all of the profits that Legend earned from commercializing its research. Liu persuaded CAS to return 35 percent of the profits to Legend. They were to be distributed according to the following formula: 35 percent to the 21 "core" founders; 20 percent to key staff; and the remaining 45 percent to senior managers. In practice, the profits went to an entity called the Employee's Shareholding Society, which held the money in trust. At first the members of the shareholding society could not benefit completely, since they did not actually own the shares themselves. Later money accumulated in this fund was used to purchase actual shares in the parent company when this became legal. This arrangement allowed the senior colleagues to look forward to a decent reward for their efforts and risks.

Later, in 1994, Legend rolled out its stock option scheme, made possible by its initial listing on the Hong Kong Stock Exchange. The scheme was critical in spreading ownership from the founding fathers to a younger generation of employees. Those employees who had been with the company for two years were eligible to join the program, in which they were given the opportunity to purchase company stock at a low, fixed price and later to resell it at a higher price. They could benefit directly from the appreciation of Legend's stock price, and a number of employees became millionaires. Initially, only 10 percent of the issued share capital could be granted to Legend employees as stock options. In 2002 the Hong Kong Stock Exchange revised the regulation to allow 30 percent of the issued share capital to be given over to stock options. Legend was the first mainland firm to allow stock options and is still one of a very small number of Chinese companies to do so. "Being listed on the Hong Kong Stock Exchange was very important to Legend and to its future development because it allowed employees to become owners in addition to the founders and early leaders," recalled a veteran staff person.

While working on the ownership problem, Liu also searched for other ways to improve his employees' lives. One was housing. In the past in China, an enterprise was supposed to provide housing at a very low rental if not for free, based on an employee's age, position and the number of children in the family. In practice, housing was inadequate and allocation a headache; many people could not get apartments large enough to accommodate a growing family. Many people spent much of the energy they might put into their work scheming to get better housing. At Legend, Liu was constantly looking for ways to improve the living conditions of his employees, which he linked with finding ways to motivate them and increasing their efficiency. In 1990, Legend built three apartment buildings with a total of 72 units. Then it set up a team to determine how they could be allocated. Each employee would be evaluated according to his or her performance, education, working years and age. Every staff member was then given a welfare fund based on these scores. In theory, this money could be used to buy a house, renovate a house or even take a vacation trip. In practice, it could not be used to buy a house because there were none to be bought – they were all owned by the government.

Knowing that the central and local governments were contemplating property reform, Legend approached the Beijing municipal government and persuaded them to use Legend as a pilot program. After several rounds of negotiations, it was finally agreed that the 72 apartments built by Legend could be sold to individuals at market value. Because most employees had not yet accumulated enough money in the welfare fund to buy the houses outright, Legend discussed with the Construction Bank of China obtaining mortgage loans for them. Talks were successful, but in the environment of the time, nothing was simple. The local property bureau had no idea how to grant a deed (technically a "property certificate") to a private individual. They had never done it before, and nobody knew exactly how to determine the proper price. Finally the Beijing municipal government promulgated a set of special policies for Legend and provided guidance to the Equity Department and Beijing Municipal Property Bureau by which a solution was reached.

Having solved the external issues, Legend polished the internal mechanisms for allocating housing. It was decided that all employees would have an equal right to apply for a house based on their need and ability to pay. Though it seemed complicated, the process worked smoothly and without generating ill-feelings. In the end, all 72 apartments were allocated to younger employees, because they had the greater need and because they were not afraid to take on a mortgage. Older employees still preferred to save their welfare funds for retirement; improving their living conditions was less important. All of this became headline news in China. Newspapers recognized the housing scheme as a landmark in property reform, and it showed again that Legend was at the forefront of social and economic change in China.

It took somewhat longer to evolve Legend's embryonic profit-sharing scheme into one in which employees had real ownership in the company. At the time there were no rules and regulations on ownership, and no government department wanted to take on the responsibility of making a decision. The notion of a "management buy out", popular in the West, was unknown. Indeed, Chinese banks imposed numerous restrictions on any kind of personal loans, especially those for investing in shares. A key pass along the long march to change was crossed in 1997. At the Congress of the Chinese Communist Party, the then Party General Secretary, Jiang Zemin, announced new guidelines governing private enterprise. For the first time, the party announced that private ownership would be officially permitted.

As Jiang put it, the state would retain a dominant position of public ownership while simultaneously developing other forms of ownership. But it was not until 1999, at the next party congress plenum, that two key amendments to the national Constitution were proposed and ratified. One inserted the words "multiple forms of ownership" into the document. The other recognized the "private economy" as an important constituent of the socialist market economy. Only then could the founders legally own shares in the company. After months of negotiation, the government finally allowed Legend founders to buy their shares, using money that had accumulated in the members' shareholding company. This special approval was another milestone. Legend became the first state enterprise to privatize its ownership. The actual certificates were transferred in November 2001, eight years after Liu began the process.

15. The Young Talents

Liu's success in addressing the ownership issue, long though it was in coming, allowed senior managers to begin turning over power to a younger generation. As far back as 1994, Liu had put Yang Yuanqing in charge of computer operations, even though Yang was only 29 at the time. In April 2001, Liu turned the entire operation over to Yang, retaining for himself only the position of chairman. He did this even though he himself was only 57, comparatively young for a Chinese business leader. Today the average age of senior managers at Legend is 35. Such a young age is not unusual in the technology industry worldwide, but it is remarkable in China, where deference to elders is deeply ingrained in the culture. Transferring power to somebody as young as Yang is still practically unheard of in other Chinese companies, especially state enterprises where for the most part the ownership question has yet to be addressed.

The difficulties that Legend encountered in 1993 caused Liu to realize that Legend could not succeed under the same leadership and business culture that it had relied on to that point. The founders were getting older and lacked the sharp instincts and boundless energy the fast-moving IT industry required. He also knew that he had the talent available. The younger team was doing a great job; all he had to do was to instill responsibility.

The first generation of Chinese entrepreneurs, men and women like Chairman Liu Chuanzhi, started at the very beginning of the reform period. They experienced the entire transition from a planned economy to a market economy. They struggled to survive in a confusing, transitional environment ill defined by rules and regulations. The founders of the largest Chinese IT companies came up at the same time and were responsible for the formation of a core of capable and energetic second-generation leaders. Liu's ability to attract, train, motivate and promote such people is, well, legendary. He tended to pick enterprising and loyal people: "I hope they will connect their life to Legend, as I have." One foreign executive noticed that Liu's staff was noteworthy for its dedication. Often people worked evenings and weekends, something almost unheard of in a state-owned enterprise.

Shares and stock options became sources of motivation but Liu endeavored to instill a deeper motivation. He expected his top managers to come to Legend with something more than just a desire for advancement and reward. He wanted them to have a desire to serve the company and the vision and enterprise needed to turn Legend into an international enterprise. This desire came from a real sense that the company's future and the future of the employees were linked, that if the company did well, they did well also. Such motivation was one of the criteria that Liu used to choose his leaders. He first evaluated their ability to put the company first, and then he evaluated their talent and ability, including their ability to learn. He wanted staff who could learn from others, learn from foreign companies and learn from their mistakes. Success or failure in any particular task was not so important as learning from that failure.

The chairman wanted his core managers to be cooperative and proactive. "The team leaders should have self-discipline and ensure that the management team will not split into factions. They should also facilitate discussion, decision and implementation." Of course, more is expected of core managers than those at other levels. Legend's view was that the primary staff should be responsible for their work; middle managers should have that kind of responsibility plus the drive and potential to advance; and senior or core managers should have all of these attributes plus a strong sense of calling.

Liu believed in developing senior executives from inside the company rather than recruiting them from outside. Some have thus referred to Legend as a "family enterprise without a family", a view which Liu considers high praise though somewhat inaccurate. In a family enterprise people are not necessarily promoted on their merits, whereas Legend's leaders are all selected based on performance and capability. Yang Yuanqing is a case in point. Liu chose Yang because he believed that he had vision, because he appreciated and admired the efforts of the first generation, and because he was a leader. Liu then transferred authority and responsibility to Yang step by step.

Another Legend executive on whom Liu conferred considerable power at a young age was Guo Wei. He came to Legend in 1987 when he was 24 with an MBA degree from the Graduate School of the Chinese Academy of Sciences. He impressed Liu with his success in planning an important conference to communicate with journalists and government officials. Liu made him head of the company's public relations department. Public relations was a new concept to Chinese people at the time, but welcomed by the local media, who, eager to spotlight the reform movement, were seeking fresh stories. Guo had more than his share and was happy to provide them. Soon such stories as "New Star Rising on Electric Street" began to appear, publicizing the scientists who had left the ivory tower to open a company. Legend and Liu have remained a favorite subject of the Chinese and international media ever since.

Guo became Liu's friend and adviser, gaining a reputation for his ability to work with people. In 1997, he took over the foreign brand distribution and systems integration business, restructuring all of the departments and distribution channels for foreign brands. In the fiscal year 1998/99, revenue from the foreign distribution business, based almost entirely on major global brands, had increased 57 per cent to HK$3,718 million (about US$477 million). Guo became the chief executive of this arm of Legend when it was spun off as an independent entity, named Digital China.

Yang believes Legend's ability to build an ever more highly qualified team emanates from a spirit imbedded within the company, one that has now been harnessed by a strong human resource management system meant to help each employee reach his or her full potential: "Put it all together, a sound enterprise culture, training, encouragement and welfare." Going forward, Legend will not be able to count forever on Liu's genius for attracting and picking talent, but his spirit is rooted deeply in the company's approach to human resource management and development, and that spirit could live in Legend for a very long time.

16. Management with Chinese Characteristics

Stock options and opportunities for advancement now made Legend an attractive place to work, but the company's management still faced the need to maintain and nurture the dedication that had motivated the founders. During his 18 years at the helm, Chairman Liu had time to seriously consider this problem, and to apply to it a synthesis of lessons he had absorbed from Chinese experience as well as from the West. He admits that at first he preferred a "top-down" style. He gave the orders and others followed them. It was a management style people expected and were accustomed to. The idea that direction always comes from the top is deeply imbedded in Chinese thinking, both from thousands of years of feudalism and 50 years of communism. People rely on their superiors to tell them what to do and are not inclined to be original and flexible. This approach is not without its merits. In Legend's case, Liu probably did have a better understanding of what needed to be done than those working for him, at least for a while.

But Liu learned in time that the more Legend grew, the less this was true; the top-down style of management was too crude to run a growing, high technology business. In the early 1990s many talented young people had joined Legend, and Liu had to change his management style. He called his new approach the "self-engine" model. Previously he had discussed business matters with his subordinates to gain their opinions but had left the final decisions to himself. He shifted to a participatory style in which his employees would present a plan and he would provide his input. This approach gradually empowered the younger generation to take over strategic decision making. This conscious change came after many of the internal troubles of Legend's early years, particularly an incident in which one of Liu's younger employees had taken money from gangsters and done their bidding. (After serving time in prison, the young man was allowed to return to the company). Liu realized that a larger company with employees from diverse backgrounds did not lend itself to dictatorship. If energy was to radiate up as well down and not be siphoned off here and there, people needed standards; the company needed rules.

Liu and his colleagues had no experience with corporate culture beyond their own and no management training beyond what they were learning on the job. To encourage themselves to work together in confronting the different issues they faced, they started creating slogans. The early history of Legend was filled with these big wall-poster-style inspirational sayings so characteristic of Chinese motivational thinking.

In their early days the scientists thought of themselves as having "shiye xin", or career ambition. They described their initial corporate culture as "chuangye jingshen", or entrepreneurial spirit. These terms capture the sense of excitement and devotion that drove them. They worked long hours under difficult circumstances because they were fired up by a sense of mission. Here are some of the other slogans that Legend grew by:

"*Turn five percent hope into one hundred percent reality*". Legend was confronted with the difficulty of operating in an environment where there were few if any rules and no model to follow. This slogan was designed to urge employees to be creative. It also had a particular application when, in 1989, the Legend Chinese-character card gained only second place in a national competition. Feeling that the experts did not understand it and knowing the benefits that accrued to first place, such as bank loans, government support, promotional advantages and so on, they asked for reconsideration. They worked for one month to convince twenty experts and were eventually given first place.

"One percent failure of a part will cause one hundred percent failure of the whole". This slogan promoted greater attention to quality control.

"Research and development stands on the shoulders of giants". This slogan was a reminder that their technological developments were based on advances made in the West.

"Look at the painting from the outside". The idea here is that being too close to one's work was not healthy. Liu frequently reminded his people that an entrepreneur must be able to think broadly and be able to adopt various viewpoints; being too inward and subjective threatened the company.

Wang Xiaoyan had worked at both state-owned and private enterprises before joining Legend in 1994, so she is in a good position to describe the unique business culture that she found there. "At state-owned enterprises there was fairness and equality among the employees, but there was no real system for running the business on a daily basis," she remembered, "At the private companies, there were systems in place but no trust between the employer and the employees, and the atmosphere depressed me. During my interview at Legend, I felt secure that it was a large, stable firm. More importantly, I felt that at Legend people were treated equally and fairly." She found the atmosphere at Legend to be efficient, strict and business-like, and also technologically oriented. "There were rules. For example, before lunch workers could not leave their desks, even for just a few minutes; they had to stay focused on the job at all times." She was surprised to learn that Legend had a strong research culture. "People assume that "xia hai" (jumping into the sea, literally leaving the state sector) meant focusing only on business, but I found that at Legend, we were expected to write a technical thesis once a month."

In reflecting on the growth of Legend and the development of his own corporate philosophy, Chairman Liu always credits his relationships with foreign partners with teaching him the theory and practice of Western business management. Having no Chinese models to rely on, Liu imported Legend's from the West. But, just as Legend modified computers to meet local conditions, so Liu adapted Western corporate models to reflect Chinese culture. He eventually synthesized his ideas into a three-part management theory:

The first component of Liu's theory of effective management is a core management team that cooperates and is proactive. The team leaders should have self-discipline, taking special care to ensure that the management team not split into factions. They should facilitate discussion, decision and implementation.

The second component is clear and practicable strategies. By formulating three-year medium-term targets, Legend developed a perspective on what it should do and what it should not do. Short-term goals could be set and a plan of implementation devised. During implementation, assessment and adjustment could continue against criteria established by the goals. The process of formulating a strategy requires study of patterns of industrial development, market conditions and other external factors. It also involves study of the enterprise, with focus on such critical components of its makeup such as capital, human resources, and technological strengths.

The third component is leadership that has a strong strategic sense and ability to build and motivate a team. In Liu's view, "The business world is similar to a battlefield. An army cannot win by excellent tactics alone if the soldiers do not have the motivation or the combat power. Therefore it is not enough for an enterprise to formulate business tactics. An enterprise needs to have quality staff and good organizational structure." He goes on to say that creating this kind of team work requires establishing an incentive system, building a corporate culture that encourages staff loyalty and motivates employees, establishing rules and guidelines that allow staff members to progress at the same pace, and providing training opportunities whereby employees can enhance their abilities.

But Chinese business culture has qualities that make it different from Western businesses. Foremost is the fundamental reliance on personal relationships to accomplish things. The Western style is grounded on law and contracts. Strangers can do business quite readily in the West, so long as they have a contract they can work within. In China, contract and other aspects of commercial law are still being developed. More importantly, the Chinese feel a great need to establish and maintain a relationship with those with whom they do business, and they spend a great deal of time and effort on this process. Liu's management philosophy places a strong emphasis on "family touch" culture, with the intent of promoting care for others and a sense of community. Under his tutelage, Legend sought to foster respect for each employee's good points and trust between the company and the staff across different departments.

Liu's success is generally attributed to his interpersonal skills and unique techniques for managing change. That approach was also very Chinese. Liu was very patient and could wait for change to happen. He would tell his staff that they could not push too hard. To be too aggressive would create disequilibrium and bring about failure. Rather, his technique was to push for change then wait for a new balance in the environment, then push again. There is a saying in China that if a tree in a forest is too much taller than the surrounding trees, the wind will destroy it first. Liu was a pioneer but tried not to go too far in advance of others. Indeed, in his view, he was very cautious – when going in a new direction, he would first takes 20 steps to see if the ground was firm before he began to run.

Liu was sometimes frustrated by investors' attitudes toward Legend. When addressing them, he often found that they were overly concerned with short-term projections and marginal changes in revenues or sales, or even in the company's political connections. He felt strongly that Legend did not achieve what it had through connections but through its own internal efforts. He preferred investors to take a longer view and study the strengths of Legend, including its strong management and corporate culture. He wanted people to think of Legend as a house in which the roof was the business, the foundation was the culture and the walls were the management. But one cannot judge the quality of the house by looking at the roof alone. Liu wanted them to examine the foundation and walls to truly know the house's structural worthiness.

Mary Ma often echoes Liu's frustration with foreign investors' inability to understand what makes Legend tick. She says she is constantly asked why Legend doesn't just buy technology or merge with a foreign company to make itself bigger and stronger in the Chinese market. "They imagine that R&D is Legend's critical shortcoming. We've told them many times that actually the team and the corporate culture are the critical strengths of the company, but they don't believe it. We argue this with investors on every roadshow. They wonder, 'why does Mary say again and again how the management can make a difference?' They don't understand it. My solution is to let them watch for another ten years."

17. The Digital Spinoff

In April 2000, after carefully evaluating the current situations and future prospects of Legend's various businesses, Liu decided to split the company into two essentially independent entities. Legend Group would remain responsible for the computers and other manufactured products, software and the Internet business. A new company called Digital China would handle distribution of foreign brands, systems integration, and the new networking business. Guo Wei, then 38, was placed in charge of Digital China, while Yang Yuanqing remained the chief executive of the Legend Group as before.

On April 20, 2001, Legend held a big ceremony in Beijing to officially kick off the 2001/02 fiscal year. At the ceremony, Chairman Liu handed flags of Legend and Digital China over to Yang and Guo respectively, a remarkably symbolic move to show the world that his 16-year journey to build up the most successful IT company in China had come to a perfect climax with the passing of the torch to a younger generation. He remained president of the mother company, Legend Holdings, and the chairman of the Legend Group and Legend Venture Capital. He took no position in Digital China.

The decision to spin off Digital China was made largely in anticipation of China's joining the World Trade Organization (WTO). It allowed the Legend Group to focus more sharply on its original business. "Restructuring was our response to the challenge of the Internet and WTO entry," Liu said at the time. "Legend and

Digital China have different business focuses and stock ratios; the shareholders expected us to divide them."

The next logical move was to float Digital China on the Hong Kong Stock market. This took place in June 2001, raising about HK$373 million for the company. Digital China thus came into being girded for the competition that WTO would bring. From Legend it inherited the largest and most efficient dealer network in the Chinese IT industry. Legend had put in a tremendous amount of effort into developing dealer relationships, into setting up a comprehensive system of internal checks and balances and into developing procedures to ensure transparency and fairness. Digital China's deep relationships with local institutions also gave the company a head start on foreign rivals.

Using these advantages, Digital China set out to consolidate its position. One of its first and most important moves was to build relations with local banks. China's WTO entry did not mean that international banks would be granted full access to local financial markets immediately but China's financial institutions already saw the writing on the wall. Digital China has formed partnerships with various government-owned banks to develop online payment solutions.

Going forward, Guo feels confident that Digital China had at least a three-year advantage over its foreign competitors, especially the major international players Commerce One and Ariba, because Digital China's was already the most efficient network in China. Building an equivalent would be difficult. "The distribution business is not as scaleable as outsiders might think. It will take many years for any global player to develop such a network."

Guo's vision is to develop Digital China into the Chinese IT industry's largest business-to-business vertical marketplace. He has two parallel strategies to meet this goal: e-channel and e-solutions.

According to Liu, "Digital China's strategy is to become a dominant local distribution expert in China. If our strength can reach every corner of China, and our service is seamless, rivals will incorporate us into their global B2B marketplace as a regional distribution service provider. It would not be wise for them to compete with us."

Looking back, Chairman Liu cites five major accomplishments in shepherding the Legend family of companies through its founding period: competing successfully in the computer market and ending foreign domination of computer sales in China; realizing the commercialization of technology – the original mission; finding solutions to the questions of ownership by transforming a state-owned company into a share-holding firm; formulating a successful management strategy and building a qualified team capable of taking over.

Accomplishing the last of these tasks has allowed Liu to step down from day-to-day management. Semi-retired, he is nonetheless involved. As chairman of the Legend Group, he plays the role of the producer – setting the direction of the company – to Yang's role as director. At Legend Venture Capital, he is both producer and director. There he still plays a more active role, making strategic plans and executing strategies. He believes that China needs to develop more entrepreneurs both young and genuine, and he hopes to help create them with timely investments. In China it is still difficult for high technology companies to break into the market because of lack of capital. New companies are forced to follow the same tortuous path as Legend, moving from basic manufacturing to technology development. New companies also know very little about management. Through his venture capital company, which can help with management guidance as well as capital, Liu believes he can influence the future industrialization of technology by nurturing and guiding these new companies. He believes in investing in the basic strengths of a company, based on the business range and industry of the enterprise, the quality of the CEO, the entrepreneur, and in the quality of technology and management. Through these methods he hopes to have a more profound impact on the future development of technology in China.

Part 5

Visions of the Future

18. Legend's New World

The China of 2002 was virtually unrecognizable from the China of two decades before. When Legend was founded in 1984, governmental policy on economic reform and the opening to the outside world was new and fragile. China was hardly counted as a factor in the global economy. Only a few simple products, such as overcoats and other cheap clothing were exported. By the turn of the century, the country had become an economic powerhouse. Despite the general slowdown in the global economy and the collapse of the Internet bubble, China stood out by achieving a steady 7 per cent to 8 per cent growth rate per annum. The 7.3 per cent growth recorded in 2001 represented nearly a quarter of the world's total economic expansion that year.

China took a monumental step on December 11, 2001, when it formally joined the World Trade Organization (WTO). This historic move was significant on several levels beyond the institutional reforms and tariff reductions that Beijing agreed to follow to qualify for membership. In a way it capped – and put a lock on – the transformation that Deng Xiaoping had initiated nearly four decades ago. The WTO entry was a major victory for the forces behind the reforms and globalization, against resistance from the so-called "old liners" and those who wanted to protect vulnerable national industries.

China's entry into WTO sparked an investment boom, especially in industrial production and manufacturing. Exports boomed. In the year 2002 alone exports grew by 22 per cent, double the rate for the rest of East Asia. For Legend, China's entry into the WTO provided a more level playing field with competitors from abroad. Having confronted and overcome fierce competition from foreign branded PCs for the past ten years, Legend faced the future confidently.

In the 18 years since its founding, Legend had grown from a two-room startup into the largest and most successful technology enterprise in China. It controlled 27 per cent of China's PC market and dominating many other IT products and services. Within these years, Legend had needed to transform itself several times to meet new challenges while at the same time virtually inventing a new business model for China – the privately managed, state-owned enterprise. The Chinese computer market had grown beyond imagination. From a handful of expensive foreign models sold mostly to major government agencies it had come to comprise a vast array of tools and consumer items for a burgeoning business community and increasingly affluent public.

The dawning of the new century also brought new challenges. 1997 to 2001 had been gravy years for Legend and for the Chinese computer industry as a whole. The market was growing by more than 40 per cent annually. In 1997, Legend had overtaken foreign competitors to become the number one PC seller in China. Legend had achieved this through its deep understanding of the local market and China's unique business environment, through its extensive distribution network, low operating and manufacturing costs, and by acquiring an advanced information system to support efficient operations. The company had focused its efforts on producing, promoting and selling personal computers to a mass market. But the years of rapid growth in the industry had also spawned a highly centralized hierarchy and bureaucratic culture. Lots of people were titled "general manager", which resulted in an increasingly cumbersome and multi-layered reporting system. It had also permitted complacency in the ranks. Doubling or tripling their sales targets every year had become relatively easy for many managers in the industry. In such circumstances, it was easy to ignore or misread negative signals coming from the market.

Then came the bursting of the Internet bubble in 2001. The computer market slowed down, from 50 per cent growth in the third quarter of 2000 to about 15 per cent during the same period in 2001. Many of the leading global IT companies reported declines in profits. No matter how hard the sales managers worked, they could not come close to meeting their target sales. Legend reported its first-half results for the financial year 2001/02 with a 10 percent growth in sales. But for the first time investors, who had higher expectation of the company, were disappointed. As its stock price languished, they began to ask questions about where the company's future growth was going to come from.

The management had, in fact, been thinking about new strategies and new engines of growth, but it took the decline in profits to galvanize the company's managers to make the necessary transformation. Faced with the challenges, Legend had to contemplate big changes to re-ignite and maintain growth. The company made a thorough study of its existing businesses and of the market environment before launching a major transformation: Legend needed to deliver more value to its customers; to be able to do so it needed to change itself from a company that made products to one that produced both products and services – in particular applications for new technologies; to make such a transformation it would have to increase its investment in research and development.

CEO Yang Yuanqing was convinced that some elements in the original culture of the company would be the main obstacle to the changes necessary to accomplish this transformation; therefore, he needed to adjust the corporate culture and instill a sense of urgency. The technology downturn in early 2001 provided just the impetus he needed. Yang set about to orient the company's core values in the new direction, drafting new guidelines for appropriate attitude and behavior, both towards customers and among employees. The management style at Legend had been quite formal, strict and demanding; people were disciplined, well-organized and submissive, as in a very typical Chinese manufacturing company. In such an environment, operations were efficient but people lacked creativity. This kind of semi-military culture had worked for Legend in the past, however, it was inappropriate for future development. The hierarchical structure made communication difficult; decision-makers lacked much needed information from the market. Yang believed that if the goal of becoming a service-oriented, technology-focused and internationally competitive corporation was to be achieved some changes had to be made.

A flatter and leaner structure was encouraged. Power was decentralized and reporting layers were minimized. This helped to enhance direct communication and enable all staff to get closer to the company's customers. Closer contact with customers meant that one could better understand their needs and respond more quickly to changes in the market. Yang believed that a friendlier, more caring and more nurturing work environment was imperative. He wanted to institute what he called a "family touch" feeling among employees; a feeling that people belong to the same family. To accomplish this, Yang instituted a policy that everyone would address one another, including himself, by first name rather than by official title. "Call me Yuanqing" was posted on a board at the main entrance of the building. "Everyone who came in the office had to call me by my first name, otherwise they were not allowed to get in the building,"

Yuanqing recalls. "Afterwards, if any staff called me by my official title, their superior would be fined ten Chinese yuan. That was tough, but the ultimate goal was to nurture a friendlier and more casual culture." Each employee was required to define clearly his or her customer focus, as well as to redefine his or her responsibilities based on customer requirements, and to submit regularly reports and share stories about customer experiences.

In June 2000, Legend held four "Family Touch Forums" throughout the company to help spread the culture of "family touch". At each forum a member of the President's Office acted as the host. Through these forums senior management had a chance to listen to employees, understand their feelings and thinking, and field ideas that they thought might contribute to building a new corporate culture. Most felt that the interchange was fruitful, and staff members appreciated the opportunity to voice their feelings and concerns. In addition Legend instituted an electronic suggestion box, "the Progress Mailbox", to which staff could e-mail their comments, suggestions, ideas, and problems encountered during work. To enhance transparency and communication among employees, Legend created personal web pages on which the staff's personal information, job responsibilities, recent major duties can be found. These changes helped harmonize the company's rigorous management style and lay the foundations for a new Legend.

But if this new culture was to become meaningful it had to embrace the company's customers. The main message that Yang had been promulgating at internal meetings, seminars and via internal e-mails was that Legend no longer was a product-driven company; it was becoming a technological service company as well. The senior management was constantly looking for better ways to address customer needs so that it might tailor products and services to meet their needs. Senior managers, including Yang himself, went to shops to serve behind the sales counter, listening to what customers had to say. In the current environment, "everybody needs to be a sales person," Yang once stated. As an example, he held up Legend's in-house patent consultant. The man, who was used to dealing only with patent issues, was sent to one of Legend's outlets to sell products for one day. "This person successfully marketed to our customers by illustrating the differences between our patents, which are rich in technological improvements, versus other companies' patents, which focus on minor cosmetic factors or differences. After this one-day, with first-hand sales experience, the patent consultant came back and wrote a detailed note with his inputs to share with our sales team. Consequently, some of his input became very effective selling points that our sales force has adopted and is now using."

The company also set up a call center where managers could listen in on calls from customers. That way they could hear for themselves what customers were looking for or complaining about, what their problems and concerns were, and how products could be improved. Yang also implemented what he called the "case study" year. Staff members, like the patent officer, were encouraged to submit cases on their experiences in dealing with customers. Those cases were posted on the company's intranet so that everyone could read them. It began with examples of successful customer relations so that everyone could absorb and meditate on them and thus find a way to better serve their customers. All these efforts were aimed at developing its service business, which the company's management intended to become an important growth engine for Legend.

19. Legend in Transformation

By the time Liu Chuanzhi handed over the leadership of the company to Yang Yuanqing, Legend had already become one of the top ten brands in China. The legendary story of a Chinese company beating all its powerful multinational competitors had became well known to the Chinese public. The media devoted a great deal of attention to every move the company made, with many of the stories getting headline billing. Government officials who wanted to showcase the emergence of China's economic power to visiting scholars and diplomats regularly pointed to Legend as an example. International recognition followed. Liu Chuanzhi, the founding father, was ranked one of the "Best Asian Business Leaders" by *Forbes* Magazine in 2000 and one of the "Most Influential Worldwide Business Leaders" by *Time* magazine in 2001. Yang Yuanqing, the leader of next generation, was feted a "Star of Asia" by *Business Week* in 2001.

When Yang took office as president, he was determined to take the company to the next level of success. Yet, he had to face many new challenges. After so many golden years of growth, the market had matured. PC penetration had reached a reasonable level relative to the purchasing power of individual consumers and corporate clients. Given Legend's dominant market position, it was becoming more and more difficult to sustain the exceptionally high growth Legend had experienced. Following China's accession to WTO, which has brought fundamental changes to Chinese society, the PC market had become more diversified, more sophisticated and therefore more demanding. At the same time, foreign competitors, leveraging their overwhelming success in most part of the world, had started their aggressive expansion in China. The company would need to follow quickly changes in its corporate culture and business with appropriate strategies.

It did not take too long before Yang came up with something. First, a three-tiered-business diversification plan would be carried out. The company's product portfolio would expand from simple PCs to multiple information terminal devices. From making mostly front-end devices and equipment such as PCs, it would also move to a wider range, to include back-end products such as servers and networking equipment. Lastly, Legend would no longer merely sell products; it would also provide solutions.

Second, technological innovation would become the company's strength. When asked about the competition from other international players, Yang said, "We have different models and strategies. Our strength is to differentiate ourselves with other IT companies and to develop products with unique features through our innovative application technologies." Already in 2000, the company had begun to increase its investment in R&D significantly. A two-layer R&D capability has since been established, with the Legend Research Institute focusing on corporate-level, forward-looking technologies and various product R&D facilities focusing on the specific needs of each business division. The R&D team expanded, recruiting a large number of engineers with extensive experience working aboard. The investment and effort soon started to bear fruit. In 2002 August, the company launched a self-developed supercomputer, the Legend Deepcom 1800 Supercomputer. This was the first computer in China to achieve a computing speed of 1,000 GFLOPS (Giga Floating Operations Per Second), an achievement that placed it 43rd on the global top 500 supercomputer list. In November 2003, the company's Deepcom 6800 Supercomputer was ranked 14th on the global list.

Third, collaboration would become the company's hallmark. In December 2002, Legend organized its first Innovation Convention, "Legend World 2002". Tackling the problems of discrete applications and difficulties attendant to the sharing of resources among information devices, Legend rolled out "Collaborating Applications", the concept was once again generative: *(1) Collaborating Applications for personal information terminal devices:* by using a standard protocol, different personal terminals and devices such as electrical appliances, telecommunications products and computers could be functionally connected to shared resources and complementary services. *(2) Collaborating Applications for corporate IT systems*: by applying the standard protocol across systems, businesses could optimize the sharing of resources among information systems, while also achieving economies of scale in the use of internal resources. *(3) Collaborating Applications for communal information systems:* by designing their worldwide IT infrastructure and application resources under established rules and standards, IT service providers would be able to provide enterprises, organizations and individuals with applications and services in a one-stop fashion.

Collaborating Applications has become the guiding principle of Legend's technology strategy, with major R&D efforts being made around it. A year after it was rolled out, Collaborating Applications was already being employed in new products. In November 2003, Legend launched the world's first home Collaborating PC, the "Tianjiao Avantia". With an automatic wireless collaborating feature, it realized the discretionary combination of functions among computers, home appliances and other terminal devices. CEO Yang said, "Embedded with Legend's self-developed 'Collaborating Applications' technologies, 'Tianjiao Avantia' is the first to officially realize wireless connectivity of PCs with home appliances and other terminal devices. For the first time, the PC is playing a major role in the living room, fully demonstrating its status in the digital home. It denotes not only a new era in home PC applications but also the commercialization of the 'digital home' concept in China."

In order to promote the concept of Collaborating Applications, Legend launched a nation-wide technology roadshow in China, called the "Lenovo Tech Show" in July 2003. The roadshow toured across the country, covering over 30 cities in six months, reaching more than 50,000 participants and making a strong impact among local governments and IT circles.

While developing collaborating products, Legend also joined industry partners to set industrial standards. In mid-July of 2003, the Science and Technology Department of the Ministry of Information Industry of China, together with Legend and four other major enterprises established the Intelligent Grouping and Resources Sharing Standardization (IGRS) Working Group. The working group was formed based on the common vision of "connectivity" as the technology development trend of the future. It is an open, non-profit organization adopting a membership system that enterprises engaged in computers, electrical appliances or information industries, and scientific research institutes are eligible to join. By January of 2004, 15 companies had formally joined the Working Group, with another 11 companies having applied for membership. Through the IGRS Legend shared its achievements in Collaborating Applications with other manufacturers, and it was expected that various manufacturers would start to launch products under the IGRS standard. Legend also joined the Digital Home Working Group, a movement originated by multinational manufacturers, including Intel, Microsoft and Sony. It was the only Chinese IT enterprise participating in this latter grouping and thus well placed to continue its work for national as well as international standards in the future.

For Yang, only one block was still missing in this construct. The fourth and final dimension of his vision lay in another realm: The time had come for the company to look beyond its middle kingdom; future development required international expansion. Going abroad for business when China's own economy was booming was no less daring and arguably more controversial than changing the way the company related to products, services, innovation and technological standards. Yang and his young, ambitious team believed that overseas expansion was essential to achieving their long-term growth objectives. At the same time, however, they saw expanding outside of China to be a gradual process that required very careful planning. The company would go step by step. One of the first things to do was to change the company's international branding.

20. The Birth of Lenovo

April 28, 2003, was not an auspicious day for a Chinese company to introduce a new brand name and logo. Earlier that day the Chinese government had announced that over 2000 cases of a virulent form of pneumonia, "Severe Acute Respiratory Syndrome" or SARS, had now been confirmed in the country; all government institutions, companies and schools were in a state of emergency; most people were avoiding public gatherings.

Launch of Legend's new logo and international brand name was of such strategic significance that it could not be easily delayed. For a company that took pride in its ability to overcome adversity, moreover, rising to the moment's challenge was of immense symbolic importance. Legend would adjust to the pandemic and push on. Albeit on a smaller scale, the ceremony went ahead at the company's headquarters in Beijing; a press conference was held online. The launch attracted immense attention – some 400 journalists from over 20 cities, including Hong Kong, which was also gripped by the SARS crisis.

At the press conference, the most frequently asked question was "why change it?" CEO Yang's answer was to the point, "If we are to go outside of China, we need to have a brand name that can be used unrestrictedly in markets worldwide. But others have already registered the original non-Chinese brand name, 'Legend', in many countries. We have no choice but to design and register a new one.

This new name, 'Lenovo,' is the first step we must take to prepare for our future international move."

The new logo is a combination of Lenovo and the two Chinese characters "lian" and "xiang". Lian Xiang is a transliteration of Legend. Lenovo is a new word, coined from "novo", a Latin word meaning innovation or novelty and "le" a prefix that echoes the original name. In Chinese, the company's brand name remains "Lian Xiang", which is profoundly rooted in the heart and soul of the company's Chinese customers and staff.

In the old logo, underneath the two Chinese characters appeared a square device that resembled an old-style floppy diskette. To distance the company from the perception that it remains solely a PC manufacturer, this device is not included in the new logo.

The branding change that began on April 28th would take a year to complete. During that period the new logo and international name would have to replace the old on all products; and all the specialty shops, channels, office spaces and advertisements would have to adopt them, and the new themes that accompanied them.

The logo change had been carefully planned, a reputable international brand consultancy firm having been engaged to assist the internal marketing team. Branding strategy must first be worked out to match the company's business orientation and reflect its vision. The existing brand management system must also be reinvented. Extensive market surveys need to be commissioned. All of the senior management needs to be interviewed. And finally numerous drafting meetings need to be held. It proved to be an exhaustive, and exhausting, series of tasks.

The logo change took many market observers by surprise, but for those involved in the task the change was the result of a painstaking process, the culmination of many months of hard work. The watershed moment in the process was the decision made to stick to a single-brand structure. One brand name would cover various product ranges, with the brand attributes carefully defined to cater to needs of each individual business and to the group as a whole. "Trustworthy", "innovative and energetic", offering "superior professional services" and "easy to use" were recognized as attributes common to the needs of all. Some of these attributes were already well recognized and some would have to be reinforced going forward. A series of advertising campaigns were launched to promote the new brand. One commercial released by the company was a classic that touched the hearts of many Chinese people. On October 18, 2003, as the entire country watched on television the replay of China's successful launch of its first manned spacecraft, "Shenzhou No. 5," a television commercial featuring the company's new logo and slogan also debuted. "To change the world by ideas" flashed in Chinese into living rooms around the country. The commercial was a great success. In the words of the CEO of a reputable Chinese company, "Right now, we need that kind of spirit and ideal to encourage ourselves. Only if we try is it possible to surpass powerful competitors. Legend is a model for Chinese companies. The spirit and ideal of Legend have inspired many of us."

21. "Faster, Higher, Stronger"

On April 1, 2004, a year after introducing its new brand name "Lenovo", the company formally changed its company name from "Legend Group Limited" to "Lenovo Group Limited". One year on, management's message is getting through. Recognition of the Lenovo brand is rising. In particular, domestic reaction to the new logo and international name has shown that China's consumers are keen to see Lenovo emerge as China's first truly international brand.

Stepping into the 21st Century, China finds its economic environment changing dramatically. Privately-run and foreign invested enterprises are emerging as new drivers of the country's economic growth, posting huge demands for IT products. At the same time, China's IT market is becoming more institutionalized and its domestic companies are facing a higher level of international competition.

These changes bring challenges as well as opportunities to Lenovo. In response to both, Yang and his team have set out a new three-year plan. The new plan, announced in the Spring of 2004, focused on strategic shifts meant to address the fast-changing business environment. First, Lenovo would deepen its involvement with PC and related products to ensure that sufficient resources were allocated to its core business. Second, it would establish a customer-oriented sales model so as to cater to customer's different needs – in product applications, buying patterns, preferred ways of delivery and service requirements. On the one hand, Lenovo would further optimize its existing distribution model, enhancing the capabilities of channel partners to win and serve customers; on the other, it would establish a direct-to-customer model to cover the diversified needs of large corporations and more diverse groups of customers. Third, Lenovo would also improve its profitability by enchancing overall operational efficiency and reducing expenses.

These modifications in corporate strategy mean to enable Lenovo to improve operational efficiency while building stronger ties with customers, effectively deepening and locking-in market penetration. In Yang's view,"Through these strategic initiatives, we will provide more competitive products and services in a faster and more flexible way to better serve customer needs. At the same time, we will be able to further strengthen our competitiveness and enhance operational efficiencies."

To make sure that everyone in the Lenovo family was on the same page, these changes in corporate strategy were communicated to all staff. With them, came even more exciting news: On March 26, 2004, Lenovo announced to join the International Olympic Committee's global sponsorship program, The Olympic Partner Programme, becoming the first Chinese enterprise in Olympic history to wear this mantel. As the exclusive computing technology equipment and service provider, Lenovo will support the Olympic Organizing Committees and National Olympic Committees around the world through 2008 by providing computer equipment and services to the Turin Olympic Winter Games in 2006 and the Beijing Olympic Games in 2008.

At the grand signing ceremony in Beijing, Yang shared with all the guests, "We are very excited and proud to become The Olympic Partner. Our corporate belief in 'Innovation and Excellence' echoes the Olympic spirit of 'Faster, Higher, Stronger'. Becoming The

Olympic Partner allows us to demonstrate our products and services to the world." Lenovo's becoming The Olypmic Partner touched the hearts of not only Lenovo's own family of staff and associates, but also that of the whole country. Chinese people are now keen to see Lenovo emerge as China's first truly international brand.

Becoming an Olympic Partner caps an exciting year for Lenovo. The company's marketing makeover bears the mark of genius and one can almost be certain that it will have monumental influence on the company in coming years. Expectations on China are rising today both within and outside the country. The new "Lenovo" logo and international brand name are now in place, just in time to hoist the Olympic banner. As more opportunities lie ahead so do more challenges. Success now rests with Yang and his team. How will they lead Lenovo into the next stage? How will the legend grow? May the history of the company as written to this point be their guide.

Orchid Pavilion

Quality Books About Asia

A Small Place in the Desert

by Christopher New

ISBN 962-8783-34-3

Summer is ending when retired schoolteachers Peter Saunders and his wife Clare arrive in Cairo to begin their guided tour of Egypt. Fifty years earlier, during the Muslim Brotherhood's terrorist campaign to expel the British, Peter had served in Egypt as a young British officer. Along the way, the elderly British couple crosses paths repeatedly with an American pair, ingenuous college students whose blithe insensitivity leaves behind a trail of resentment. Tensions mount to an unsettling climax in Ismailia, where Peter's darkest memories reside. Clare discovers at last what happened fifty years ago that so shadowed his life. And the young Americans make a discovery of their own. A many-layered novel subtly balancing past and present, *A Small Place in the Desert* is at once a striking portrayal of self-discovery, love and loss, and an allusive and timely depiction of the troubled interface between the Western and the Muslim worlds.

The General and Mr Tu

by Denis Way

ISBN 962-8783-26-2

Two men, born in the Year of the Fire Horse. According to Chinese astrology, both are destined to accumulate great wealth and power. Their paths cross for the first time, tragically, in Shanghai in 1940. Then in 1949 John Huart sails into Hong Kong, confronted with the challenge of rebuilding his family's once-famous trading house, now flattened by war and revolution. On the same day, the General's sworn enemy, Tu Chien, steps off a junk laden with gold at Aberdeen. *The General and Mr Tu* tells the story of Hong Kong from the Communist victory in China through the Great Cultural Revolution and the first stock market boom. Through it all, the General and Mr Tu fight their personal blood feud from which only one will survive.

Orchid Pavilion Books

Orchid Pavilion Books is the literary imprint of Asia 2000 Ltd., Hong Kong publishers of quality books since 1980. The imprint is inspired by the *Orchid Pavilion Preface*, a treatise on life penned by Wang Xizhi, China's most famous calligrapher.

To quote from *Behind the Brushstrokes*, an Asia 2000 book by Khoo Seow Haw and Nancy Penrose:

> By 352 A.D., Wang Zizhi was 50 years old, his reputation as a calligrapher was well established, and he had served as a court minister for many years. In the late spring of that year Wang Xizhi invited 41 calligraphers, poets, relatives and friends to accompany him on an outing to Lan Ting, the Orchid Pavilion, in the city of Shaoxing, Zhejiang province. It was the time of the year for the purification ceremony, when hands and bodies were cleansed with stream water to wash away any bad luck. The group of friends and scholars sat on each side of a flowing stream, and a little cup made out of a lotus leaf, full of wine, was floated down the stream. Whenever it floated in front of someone, that person was obliged to either compose a poem on the spot or to drink the wine as forfeit if he failed to come up with a poem.
>
> By the end of the day, 37 poems had been composed by 25 scholars. Wang Xizhi, as the head of this happy occasion, picked up a brush made out of rat whiskers and hairs and wrote on the spot the greatest masterpiece of Chinese calligraphy, the *Lan Ting Xu*, or the *Orchid Pavilion Preface*. Written on silk in the outstanding style of *Xing Shu* (Walking Style), the composition contains 28 vertical rows and 324 words. It is a philosophical discourse on the meaning of life. Wang Xizhi's calligraphy in this work is full of a natural energy, inspired by the happiness and grace of the moment, brimming with refinement and elegance. The *Orchid Pavilion Preface* became the greatest piece of *Xing Shu* and, although Wang Xizhi later tried more than 100 times to reproduce the work, he was never able to match the quality of the original.